GOD'S PERSPECTIVE

60 IMPORTANT TOPICS AND WHAT GOD'S WORD SAYS ABOUT THEM

ERIC DYKSTRA

Thrill & Move Worldwide
St Paul, Minnesota

God's Perspective:
60 Important Topics and what God's Word says about Them
Copyright © 2021 by Eric Dykstra

Cover design by Tracy Keech

ISBN-13: 978-0-9960223-7-8

To all those who have questions about faith:
I pray this helps give you clarity.

INTRODUCTION:
HOW TO USE THIS BOOK

The Bible is God's thinking on any issue or topic.

2 Timothy 3:16-17 says, *"All Scripture is God-breathed and is useful for teaching, rebuking, correcting and training in righteousness, so that the servant of God may be thoroughly equipped for every good work." (NIV)*

The Bible is God's very breath. This means the words in the Bible are exactly what God thinks about any issue you can dream up.

Scripture also says, *"it is impossible for God to lie"* (Hebrews 6:18, NIV). This means the words of Scripture are truth. God can't lie to you. You can trust what is written in the Bible.

When you read the Bible, whatever the Scripture says is what God thinks about an issue, and you can build your life on what it says.

One more note:
Scripture says, *"My thoughts are not your thoughts, neither are your ways my ways,"* declares the Lord (Isaiah 55:8, NIV). So don't be surprised if your ideas don't always match up with God's! Make it your goal to adjust your thinking so you are in line with God's thoughts and He can bless your life.

The following pages are 60 alphabetized topics and a section of Scripture that addresses this topic.

What to do:

A. Go to the topic that interests you.

B. Pray and ask the Holy Spirit to explain God's perspective on this topic to you. Remember the Holy Spirit was sent to "guide you into all truth" (John 16:13, NIV), so as you read the Scripture, you can trust that the Spirit will explain it to you if you ask Him.

C. Read the Scripture included, and as you read let the Holy Spirit guide you to understand God's perspective by asking 3 important questions. Write out your answers in the space provided so you don't forget what God told you.

1. What does this Scripture tell me about what God thinks about this topic?
   ▪ God thinks…
   ▪ God is…
   ▪ God…

2. What does this Scripture tell me about people?
   ▪ People are…
   ▪ People need to…
   ▪ People…

3. How do I apply this Scripture to my life today?
   ▪ I will…

After you have written something down for all three questions, spend some time asking the Holy Spirit to empower you with strength to live out what He taught you today.

TOPICS

What does God think about...

What does God think about...
ABORTION?

Psalms 139:1-18 O Lord, you have examined my heart and know everything about me. You know when I sit down or stand up. You know my thoughts even when I'm far away. You see me when I travel and when I rest at home. You know everything I do. You know what I am going to say even before I say it, Lord. You go before me and follow me. You place your hand of blessing on my head.

Such knowledge is too wonderful for me, too great for me to understand! I can never escape from your Spirit! I can never get away from your presence! If I go up to heaven, you are there; if I go down to the grave, you are there. If I ride the wings of the morning, if I dwell by the farthest oceans, even there your hand will guide me, and your strength will support me. I could ask the darkness to hide me and the light around me to become night—but even in darkness I cannot hide from you. To you the night shines as bright as day. Darkness and light are the same to you.

You made all the delicate, inner parts of my body and knit me together in my mother's womb. Thank you for making me so wonderfully complex! Your workmanship is marvelous—how well I know it. You watched me as I was being formed in utter seclusion, as I was woven together in the dark of the womb. You saw me before I was born. Every day of my life was recorded in your book. Every moment was laid out before a single day had passed. How precious are your thoughts about me, O God. They cannot be numbered! I can't even count them; they outnumber the grains of sand! And when I wake up, you are still with me! (NLT)

A. What does this Scripture tell me about what God thinks about this topic?
- God thinks…
- God is…
- God…

B. What does this Scripture tell me about people?
- People are…
- People need to…
- People…

C. How do I apply this Scripture to my life today?
- I will…

D. Write out a prayer asking the Holy Spirit to empower you with strength to live out what He taught you today.

Grace Note:
Please remember that when people are dealing with a surprise pregnancy, they need our grace and our love in order to move towards loving this unborn child and embracing their role as a parent. Pray for people in this situation; do not condemn them. Love on them, support them, and help them in any way you can so that they can bring this beautiful child of God into the world.

ADDICTION?

Romans 6:1-23 *What shall we say, then? Shall we go on sinning so that grace may increase? By no means! We are those who have died to sin; how can we live in it any longer? Or don't you know that all of us who were baptized into Christ Jesus were baptized into his death? We were therefore buried with him through baptism into death in order that, just as Christ was raised from the dead through the glory of the Father, we too may live a new life.*

For if we have been united with him in a death like his, we will certainly also be united with him in a resurrection like his. For we know that our old self was crucified with him so that the body ruled by sin might be done away with, that we should no longer be slaves to sin—because anyone who has died has been set free from sin.

Now if we died with Christ, we believe that we will also live with him. For we know that since Christ was raised from the dead, he cannot die again; death no longer has mastery over him. The death he died, he died to sin once for all; but the life he lives, he lives to God.

In the same way, count yourselves dead to sin but alive to God in Christ Jesus. Therefore do not let sin reign in your mortal body so that you obey its evil desires. Do not offer any part of yourself to sin as an instrument of wickedness, but rather offer yourselves to God as those who have been brought from death to life; and offer every part of yourself to him as an instrument of righteousness. For sin shall no longer be your master, because you are not under the law, but under grace.

What then? Shall we sin because we are not under the law but under grace? By no means! Don't you know that when you offer yourselves to someone as obedient slaves, you are slaves of the one you obey—whether you are slaves to sin, which leads to death, or to obedience, which leads to righteousness? But thanks be to God that, though you used to be slaves to sin, you have come to obey from your heart the pattern of teaching that has now claimed your allegiance. You have been set free from sin and have become slaves to righteousness.

I am using an example from everyday life because of your human limitations. Just as you used to offer yourselves as slaves to impurity and to ever-increasing wickedness, so now offer yourselves as slaves to righteousness leading to holiness. When you were slaves to sin, you were free from the control of righteousness. What benefit did you reap at that time from the things you are now ashamed of? Those things result in death! But now that you have been set free from sin and have become slaves of God, the benefit you reap leads to holiness, and the result is eternal life. For the wages of sin is death, but the gift of God is eternal life in Christ Jesus our Lord. (NIV)

A. What does this Scripture tell me about what God thinks about this topic?
   - God thinks...
   - God is...
   - God...

B. What does this Scripture tell me about people?
- People are…
- People need to…
- People…

C. How do I apply this Scripture to my life today?
- I will…

D. Write out a prayer asking the Holy Spirit to empower you with strength to live out what He taught you today.

Grace Note:

People struggling with addiction need to know they are loved, and that the grace of Christ can set them free! If you know someone struggling with an addiction, please get them to a faith-based recovery meeting like Free Grace Recovery or Celebrate Recovery! Through the loving support of other Christians and the power of Christ, they can be set free from hurts, habits, or hang-ups.

What does God think about...
ALCOHOL & DRUGS?

Ephesians 5:6-20 *Don't be fooled by those who try to excuse these sins, for the anger of God will fall on all who disobey him. Don't participate in the things these people do. For once you were full of darkness, but now you have light from the Lord. So live as people of light! For this light within you produces only what is good and right and true.*

Carefully determine what pleases the Lord. Take no part in the worthless deeds of evil and darkness; instead, expose them. It is shameful even to talk about the things that ungodly people do in secret.

But their evil intentions will be exposed when the light shines on them, for the light makes everything visible. This is why it is said, "Awake, O sleeper, rise up from the dead, and Christ will give you light."

So be careful how you live. Don't live like fools, but like those who are wise. Make the most of every opportunity in these evil days. Don't act thoughtlessly, but understand what the Lord wants you to do.

Don't be drunk with wine, because that will ruin your life.

Instead, be filled with the Holy Spirit, singing psalms and hymns and spiritual songs among yourselves, and making music to the Lord in your hearts. And give thanks for everything to God the Father in the name of our Lord Jesus Christ. (NLT)

A. What does this Scripture tell me about what God thinks about this topic?
  - God thinks...
  - God is...
  - God...

B. What does this Scripture tell me about people?
  - People are...
  - People need to...
  - People...

C. How do I apply this Scripture to my life today?
  - I will...

D. Write out a prayer asking the Holy Spirit to empower you with strength to live out what He taught you today.

Grace Note:
The Scripture seems clear: drunkenness is a sin, and being controlled by a substance other than the Holy Spirit for recreational purposes is against the will of God. Those dealing with substance abuse need to seek out a faith-based 12-step recovery program like Free Grace Recovery or Celebrate Recovery. Reject recreational substance abuse and embrace the power of the Spirit to move your life in a healthy direction.

What does God think about...
ATHEISM?

Psalm 14:1-7 *Only fools say in their hearts, "There is no God."*

They are corrupt, and their actions are evil; not one of them does good!

The Lord looks down from heaven on the entire human race; he looks to see if anyone is truly wise, if anyone seeks God. But no, all have turned away; all have become corrupt. No one does good, not a single one!

Will those who do evil never learn? They eat up my people like bread and wouldn't think of praying to the Lord. Terror will grip them, for God is with those who obey him.

The wicked frustrate the plans of the oppressed, but the Lord will protect his people.

Who will come from Mount Zion to rescue Israel? When the Lord restores his people, Jacob will shout with joy, and Israel will rejoice. (NLT)

A. What does this Scripture tell me about what God thinks about this topic?
- God thinks…
- God is…
- God…

B. What does this Scripture tell me about people?
- People are…
- People need to…
- People…

C. How do I apply this Scripture to my life today?
- I will…

D. Write out a prayer asking the Holy Spirit to empower you with strength to live out what He taught you today.

Grace Note:

The Bible never tries to prove God's existence; it just expects you to know that it is obvious that God exists. At the same time, people go through a variety of circumstances, hardships, struggles, and pain in this world, and this makes it hard for people to trust that God is real and cares about them. Please be patient with people like this and continue to show them Jesus and His love for them. The love of Christ can break through any walls and convince people God is alive and active and that He loves them.

What does God think about...
BAPTISM?

Acts 2:32-41 *"This Jesus God has raised up, of which we are all witnesses. Therefore being exalted to the right hand of God, and having received from the Father the promise of the Holy Spirit, He poured out this which you now see and hear.*

For David did not ascend into the heavens, but he says himself: 'The LORD *said to my Lord, "Sit at My right hand, Till I make Your enemies Your footstool."' Therefore let all the house of Israel know assuredly that God has made this Jesus, whom you crucified, both Lord and Christ."*

Now when they heard this, they were cut to the heart, and said to Peter and the rest of the apostles, "Men and brethren, what shall we do?"

Then Peter said to them, "Repent, and let every one of you be baptized in the name of Jesus Christ for the remission of sins; and you shall receive the gift of the Holy Spirit. For the promise is to you and to your children, and to all who are afar off, as many as the Lord our God will call."

And with many other words he testified and exhorted them, saying, "Be saved from this perverse generation." Then those who gladly received his word were baptized; and that day about three thousand souls were added to them. (NKJV)

A. What does this Scripture tell me about what God thinks about this topic?
- God thinks...
- God is...
- God...

B. What does this Scripture tell me about people?
- People are...
- People need to...
- People...

C. How do I apply this Scripture to my life today?
- I will...

D. Write out a prayer asking the Holy Spirit to empower you with strength to live out what He taught you today.

Grace Note:

Baptism is not a requirement for salvation. It is evidence that you have committed your heart to Christ and your goal is to live your life for Him. Just like with a wedding, one commits to their spouse before the public ceremony. There is already love and commitment. However, the wedding ceremony shows to the world this love and commitment is real. This is what baptism is like. People who have already committed their hearts to Christ, but they want the world to know, publicly stand up and identify with Him as their Savior and Lord. If you have not yet been baptized, consider doing so today.

What does God think about...
BEING A MAN OF GOD?

*I **Timothy 6:11-21** But as for you, O man of God, flee these things. Pursue righteousness, godliness, faith, love, steadfastness, gentleness.*

Fight the good fight of the faith.

Take hold of the eternal life to which you were called and about which you made the good confession in the presence of many witnesses.

I charge you in the presence of God, who gives life to all things, and of Christ Jesus, who in his testimony before Pontius Pilate made the good confession, to keep the commandment unstained and free from reproach until the appearing of our Lord Jesus' Christ, which he will display at the proper time—he who is the blessed and only Sovereign, the King of kings and Lord of lords, who alone has immortality, who dwells in unapproachable light, whom no one has ever seen or can see. To him be honor and eternal dominion. Amen.

As for the rich in this present age, charge them not to be haughty, nor to set their hopes on the uncertainty of riches, but on God, who richly provides us with everything to enjoy. They are to do good, to be rich in good works, to be generous and ready to share, thus storing up treasure for themselves as a good foundation for the future, so that they may take hold of that which is truly life.

O Timothy, guard the deposit entrusted to you. Avoid the irreverent babble and contradictions of what is falsely called "knowledge," for by professing it some have swerved from the faith. Grace be with you. (ESV)

A. What does this Scripture tell me about what God thinks about this topic?
   - God thinks...
   - God is...
   - God...

B. What does this Scripture tell me about people?
   - People are...
   - People need to...
   - People...

C. How do I apply this Scripture to my life today?
   - I will...

D. Write out a prayer asking the Holy Spirit to empower you with strength to live out what He taught you today.

Grace Note:
Jesus was the ultimate man of God. At the end of the day, our goal is to look more like Christ than to look like the world. No matter your background or your struggle, no matter the pain you have been through,

Jesus wants to make you like Himself. Stay close to Him. Walk with Him. Jesus will help you become more like Himself and live out your destiny as a man of God.

What does God think about...
BEING A WOMAN OF GOD?

Proverbs 31:10-31 *A good woman is hard to find, and worth far more than diamonds. Her husband trusts her without reserve, and never has reason to regret it. Never spiteful, she treats him generously all her life long.*

She shops around for the best yarns and cottons, and enjoys knitting and sewing. She's like a trading ship that sails to faraway places and brings back exotic surprises.

She's up before dawn, preparing breakfast for her family and organizing her day. She looks over a field and buys it, then, with money she's put aside, plants a garden.

First thing in the morning, she dresses for work, rolls up her sleeves, eager to get started. She senses the worth of her work, is in no hurry to call it quits for the day.

She's skilled in the crafts of home and hearth, diligent in homemaking. She's quick to assist anyone in need, reaches out to help the poor.

She doesn't worry about her family when it snows; their winter clothes are all mended and ready to wear. She makes her own clothing, and dresses in colorful linens and silks.

Her husband is greatly respected when he deliberates with the city fathers. She designs gowns and sells them, brings the sweaters she knits to the dress shops. Her clothes are well-made and elegant, and she always faces tomorrow with a smile.

When she speaks she has something worthwhile to say, and she always says it kindly.
She keeps an eye on everyone in her household, and keeps them all busy and productive. Her children respect and bless her; her husband joins in with words of praise: "Many women have done wonderful things, but you've outclassed them all!"

Charm can mislead and beauty soon fades. The woman to be admired and praised is the woman who lives in the Fear-of-GOD. Give her everything she deserves! Adorn her life with praises! (MSG)

A. What does this Scripture tell me about what God thinks about this topic?
- God thinks…
- God is…
- God…

B. What does this Scripture tell me about people?
- People are…
- People need to…
- People…

C. How do I apply this Scripture to my life today?

- I will…

D. Write out a prayer asking the Holy Spirit to empower you with strength to live out what He taught you today.

Grace Note from Eric's wife Kelly:
This chapter isn't a list of things we have to do in order to be a godly woman. It's the external workings of a life the (male) writer observes and respects. This "Proverbs 31 woman" looks externally different for each of us; but how we live BEST flows from an internal strength that comes from walking with God.

BUSINESS OR WORK?

Ephesians 6:5-9 Bondservants, be obedient to those who are your masters according to the flesh, with fear and trembling, in sincerity of heart, as to Christ; not with eyeservice, as men-pleasers, but as bondservants of Christ, doing the will of God from the heart, with goodwill doing service, as to the Lord, and not to men, knowing that whatever good anyone does, he will receive the same from the Lord, whether he is a slave or free.

And you, masters, do the same things to them, giving up threatening, knowing that your own Master also is in heaven, and there is no partiality with Him. (NKJV)

A. What does this Scripture tell me about what God thinks about this topic?
- God thinks…
- God is…
- God…

B. What does this Scripture tell me about people?
- People are…
- People need to…
- People…

C. How do I apply this Scripture to my life today?
   ▪ I will…

D. Write out a prayer asking the Holy Spirit to empower you with strength to live out what He taught you today.

Grace Note:

Sometimes as employees we serve under harsh leaders. Keep the faith, respond with grace, and serve the Lord by serving your employer. Lots of Christians have been through this situation, and they have done it with dignity and grace and honor. You can do this. God's grace is enough. The Spirit of God lives in you, and you can honor your employer, no matter the way they treat you.

What does God think about...
CONFLICT RESOLUTION?

Matthew 18:12-17 *What do you think? If a man owns a hundred sheep, and one of them wanders away, will he not leave the ninety-nine on the hills and go to look for the one that wandered off?*

And if he finds it, truly I tell you, he is happier about that one sheep than about the ninety-nine that did not wander off.

In the same way your Father in heaven is not willing that any of these little ones should perish.

If your brother or sister sins, go and point out their fault, just between the two of you.

If they listen to you, you have won them over.

But if they will not listen, take one or two others along, so that "every matter may be established by the testimony of two or three witnesses."

If they still refuse to listen, tell it to the church; and if they refuse to listen even to the church, treat them as you would a pagan or a tax collector. (NIV)

A. What does this Scripture tell me about what God thinks about this topic?
- God thinks…
- God is…
- God…

B. What does this Scripture tell me about people?
- People are…
- People need to…
- People…

C. How do I apply this Scripture to my life today?
- I will…

D. Write out a prayer asking the Holy Spirit to empower you with strength to live out what He taught you today.

Grace Note:

At the end of this set of verses, Jesus says that if a person won't reconcile to treat them like a "pagan or a tax collector". I would remind believers that the way Jesus treated tax collectors and pagans was to love them. At the end of the day, if you cannot resolve your conflict and you followed the steps listed in the text, love this person from a distance. Speak gracefully and kindly of them. And do not give the devil a foothold with bitterness or anger. Let it go. Keep your side of the street clean and give them grace and love from a distance, even if you cannot be around them any longer.

What does God think about...

THE CRUCIFIXION?

John 19:1-37 *Then Pilate took Jesus and flogged him. And the soldiers twisted together a crown of thorns and put it on his head and arrayed him in a purple robe. They came up to him, saying, "Hail, King of the Jews!" and struck him with their hands. Pilate went out again and said to them, "See, I am bringing him out to you that you may know that I find no guilt in him." So Jesus came out, wearing the crown of thorns and the purple robe. Pilate said to them, "Behold the man!" When the chief priests and the officers saw him, they cried out, "Crucify him, crucify him!" Pilate said to them, "Take him yourselves and crucify him, for I find no guilt in him." The Jews answered him, "We have a law, and according to that law he ought to die because he has made himself the Son of God." When Pilate heard this statement, he was even more afraid. He entered his headquarters again and said to Jesus, "Where are you from?" But Jesus gave him no answer. So Pilate said to him, "You will not speak to me? Do you not know that I have authority to release you and authority to crucify you?" Jesus answered him, "You would have no authority over me at all unless it had been given you from above. Therefore he who delivered me over to you has the greater sin."*

From then on Pilate sought to release him, but the Jews cried out, "If you release this man, you are not Caesar's friend. Everyone who makes himself a king opposes Caesar." So when Pilate heard these words, he brought Jesus out and sat down on the judgment seat at a place called The Stone Pavement, and in Aramaic Gabbatha. Now it was the day of Preparation of the Passover. It was about the sixth hour. He said to the Jews, "Behold your King!" They cried out, "Away with him, away with him, crucify him!" Pilate said to them, "Shall I crucify your King?" The chief priests answered, "We have no king but Caesar." So he delivered him over to them to be crucified.

So they took Jesus, and he went out, bearing his own cross, to the place called The Place of a Skull, which in Aramaic is called Golgotha. There they crucified him, and with him two others, one on either side, and Jesus between them. Pilate also wrote an inscription and put it on the cross. It read, "Jesus of Nazareth, the King of the Jews." Many of the Jews read this inscription, for the place where Jesus was crucified was near the city, and it was written in Aramaic, in Latin, and in Greek. So the chief priests of the Jews said to Pilate, "Do not write, 'The King of the Jews,' but rather, 'This man said, I am King of the Jews.'" Pilate answered, "What I have written I have written."

When the soldiers had crucified Jesus, they took his garments and divided them into four parts, one part for each soldier; also his tunic. But the tunic was seamless, woven in one piece from top to bottom, so they said to one another, "Let us not tear it, but cast lots for it to see whose it shall be." This was to fulfill the Scripture which says, "They divided my garments among them, and for my clothing they cast lots."

So the soldiers did these things, but standing by the cross of Jesus were his mother and his mother's sister, Mary the wife of Clopas, and Mary Magdalene. When Jesus saw his mother and the disciple whom he loved standing nearby, he said to his mother, "Woman, behold, your son!" Then he said to the disciple, "Behold, your mother!" And from that hour the disciple took her to his own home.

After this, Jesus, knowing that all was now finished, said (to fulfill the Scripture), "I thirst." A jar full of sour wine stood there, so they put a sponge full of the sour wine on a hyssop branch and held it to *his mouth. When Jesus had received the sour wine, he said, "It is finished," and he bowed his head and gave up his spirit.*

Since it was the day of Preparation, and so that the bodies would not remain on the cross on the Sabbath (for that Sabbath was a high day), the Jews asked Pilate that their legs might be broken and that they might be taken away. So the soldiers came and broke the legs of the first, and of the other who had been crucified with him. But when they came to Jesus and saw that he was already dead, they did not break his legs. But one of the soldiers pierced his side with a spear, and at once there came out blood and water. He who saw it has borne witness—his testimony is true, and he knows that he is telling the truth—that you also may believe. For these things took place that the Scripture might be fulfilled: "Not one of his bones will be broken." And again another Scripture says, "They will look on him whom they have pierced." (ESV)

A. What does this Scripture tell me about what God thinks about this topic?
- God thinks...
- God is...
- God...

B. What does this Scripture tell me about people?
- People are...
- People need to...
- People...

C. How do I apply this Scripture to my life today?
    - I will…

D. Write out a prayer asking the Holy Spirit to empower you with strength to live out what He taught you today.

Grace Note:
Jesus really did physically die for your salvation. His blood paid the price so that you could be saved. Don't take it for granted. Don't let it become too familiar. Someone really did die for you. Real nails went through real hands and real feet. A real crown of thorns was placed on a real head and real blood was poured out for you to cover your sin. Maybe take a second to say thank you to Jesus. Maybe take a second to take communion and remember His broken body and shed blood. It is only through the cross that we have been made righteous and whole and forgiven. Thank you, Jesus, for your death for us.

What does God think about...
DATING/RELATIONSHIPS?

2 Corinthians 6:11-18 We have spoken freely to you, Corinthians; our heart is wide open. You are not restricted by us, but you are restricted in your own affections. In return (I speak as to children) widen your hearts also.

Do not be unequally yoked with unbelievers.

For what partnership has righteousness with lawlessness? Or what fellowship has light with darkness? What accord has Christ with Belial? Or what portion does a believer share with an unbeliever? What agreement has the temple of God with idols?

For we are the temple of the living God; as God said,

"I will make my dwelling among them and walk among them, and I will be their God, and they shall be my people. Therefore go out from their midst, and be separate from them, says the Lord, and touch no unclean thing; then I will welcome you, and I will be a father to you, and you shall be sons and daughters to me, says the Lord Almighty." (ESV)

A. What does this Scripture tell me about what God thinks about this topic?
- God thinks…
- God is…
- God…

B. What does this Scripture tell me about people?
    ▪   People are…
    ▪   People need to…
    ▪   People…

C. How do I apply this Scripture to my life today?
    ▪   I will…

D. Write out a prayer asking the Holy Spirit to empower you with
    strength to live out what He taught you today.

Grace Note:
God has a destiny for your life. The quickest way to jack that up is to connect yourself with someone that does not care deeply about the things of God. Run from people who are not focused on loving Jesus with all their heart, soul, mind, and strength. God has a person for you to connect with and be committed to that is first and foremost committed to Him. You want a partner in life that loves the Father and seeks to serve Jesus above everything else. Then you will live a healthier, more fulfilling life in unity and with less conflict.

DEALING WITH BETRAYAL?

Genesis 37:18-35 When Joseph's brothers saw him coming, they recognized him in the distance. As he approached, they made plans to kill him. "Here comes the dreamer!" they said. "Come on, let's kill him and throw him into one of these cisterns. We can tell our father, 'A wild animal has eaten him.' Then we'll see what becomes of his dreams!"

But when Reuben heard of their scheme, he came to Joseph's rescue. "Let's not kill him," he said. "Why should we shed any blood? Let's just throw him into this empty cistern here in the wilderness. Then he'll die without our laying a hand on him." Reuben was secretly planning to rescue Joseph and return him to his father.

So when Joseph arrived, his brothers ripped off the beautiful robe he was wearing. Then they grabbed him and threw him into the cistern. Now the cistern was empty; there was no water in it. Then, just as they were sitting down to eat, they looked up and saw a caravan of camels in the distance coming toward them. It was a group of Ishmaelite traders taking a load of gum, balm, and aromatic resin from Gilead down to Egypt.

Judah said to his brothers, "What will we gain by killing our brother? We'd have to cover up the crime. Instead of hurting him, let's sell him to those Ishmaelite traders. After all, he is our brother—our own flesh and blood!" And his brothers agreed. So when the Ishmaelites, who were Midianite traders, came by,

Joseph's brothers pulled him out of the cistern and sold him to them for twenty pieces of silver. And the traders took him to Egypt.

Some time later, Reuben returned to get Joseph out of the cistern. When he discovered that Joseph was missing, he tore his clothes in grief. Then he went back to his brothers and lamented, "The boy is gone! What will I do now?"

Then the brothers killed a young goat and dipped Joseph's robe in its blood. They sent the beautiful robe to their father with this message: "Look at what we found. Doesn't this robe belong to your son?" Their father recognized it immediately. "Yes," he said, "it is my son's robe. A wild animal must have eaten him. Joseph has clearly been torn to pieces!"

Then Jacob tore his clothes and dressed himself in burlap. He mourned deeply for his son for a long time. His family all tried to comfort him, but he refused to be comforted. "I will go to my grave mourning for my son," he would say, and then he would weep. (NLT)

Genesis 50:16-21 So they sent this message to Joseph: "Before your father died, he instructed us to say to you: 'Please forgive your brothers for the great wrong they did to you—for their sin in treating you so cruelly.' So we, the servants of the God of your father, beg you to forgive our sin."

When Joseph received the message, he broke down and wept. Then his brothers came and threw themselves down before Joseph. "Look, we are your slaves!" they said. But Joseph replied, "Don't be afraid of me. Am I God, that I can punish you? You intended to harm me, but God intended it all for good. He brought me to this position so I could save the lives of many people. No, don't be afraid. I will continue to take care of you and your children." So he reassured them by speaking kindly to them. (NLT)

A. What does this Scripture tell me about what God thinks about this topic?
- God thinks…
- God is…
- God…

B. What does this Scripture tell me about people?
- People are…
- People need to…
- People…

C. How do I apply this Scripture to my life today?
- I will…

D. Write out a prayer asking the Holy Spirit to empower you with strength to live out what He taught you today.

Grace Note:

Notice there is a lot of time between Genesis 37 and Genesis 50. It must've taken a while for Joseph to get over the hurt and pain of what his brothers did to him. If you are in the middle of dealing with a recent betrayal, just know that your goal is forgiveness and grace. God uses all things for good. Don't allow bitterness to grow in your soul or unforgiveness to grow in your heart. Release to God those people who have hurt you. Be relentless about telling God you forgive them by faith and let the Spirit of God fill your soul with the strength to forgive and love. If Joseph can do this, by faith so can you!

DEALING WITH GRIEF AND LOSS?

John 11:1-44 *Now a certain man was sick, Lazarus of Bethany, the town of Mary and her sister Martha. It was that Mary who anointed the Lord with fragrant oil and wiped His feet with her hair, whose brother Lazarus was sick. Therefore the sisters sent to Him, saying, "Lord, behold, he whom You love is sick."*

When Jesus heard that, He said, "This sickness is not unto death, but for the glory of God, that the Son of God may be glorified through it."

Now Jesus loved Martha and her sister and Lazarus. So, when He heard that he was sick, He stayed two more days in the place where He was. Then after this He said to the disciples, "Let us go to Judea again."

The disciples said to Him, "Rabbi, lately the Jews sought to stone You, and are You going there again?"

Jesus answered, "Are there not twelve hours in the day? If anyone walks in the day, he does not stumble, because he sees the light of this world. But if one walks in the night, he stumbles, because the light is not in him." These things He said, and after that He said to them, "Our friend Lazarus sleeps, but I go that I may wake him up."

Then His disciples said, "Lord, if he sleeps he will get well." However, Jesus spoke of his death, but they thought that He was speaking about taking rest in sleep.

Then Jesus said to them plainly, "Lazarus is dead. And I am glad for your sakes that I was not there, that you may believe. Nevertheless let us go to him."

Then Thomas, who is called the Twin, said to his fellow disciples, "Let us also go, that we may die with Him."

So when Jesus came, He found that he had already been in the tomb four days. Now Bethany was near Jerusalem, about [a]two miles away. And many of the Jews had joined the women around Martha and Mary, to comfort them concerning their brother.

Then Martha, as soon as she heard that Jesus was coming, went and met Him, but Mary was sitting in the house. Now Martha said to Jesus, "Lord, if You had been here, my brother would not have died. But even now I know that whatever You ask of God, God will give You."

Jesus said to her, "Your brother will rise again."

Martha said to Him, "I know that he will rise again in the resurrection at the last day."

Jesus said to her, "I am the resurrection and the life. He who believes in Me, though he may die, he shall live. And whoever lives and believes in Me shall never die. Do you believe this?"

She said to Him, "Yes, Lord, I believe that You are the Christ, the Son of God, who is to come into the world."

And when she had said these things, she went her way and secretly called Mary her sister, saying, "The Teacher has come and is calling for you." As soon as she heard that, she arose quickly and came to Him. Now Jesus had not yet come into the town, but was in the place where Martha met Him. Then the Jews who were with her in the house, and comforting her, when they saw that Mary rose up quickly and went out, followed her, saying, "She is going to the tomb to weep there."

Then, when Mary came where Jesus was, and saw Him, she fell down at His feet, saying to Him, "Lord, if You had been here, my brother would not have died."

Therefore, when Jesus saw her weeping, and the Jews who came with her weeping, He groaned in the spirit and was troubled. And He said, "Where have you laid him?"

They said to Him, "Lord, come and see."

Jesus wept. Then the Jews said, "See how He loved him!"

And some of them said, "Could not this Man, who opened the eyes of the blind, also have kept this man from dying?"

Then Jesus, again groaning in Himself, came to the tomb. It was a cave, and a stone lay against it. Jesus said, "Take away the stone."

Martha, the sister of him who was dead, said to Him, "Lord, by this time there is a stench, for he has been dead four days."

Jesus said to her, "Did I not say to you that if you would believe you would see the glory of God?" Then they took away the stone from the place where the dead man was lying. And Jesus lifted up His eyes and said, "Father, I thank You that You have heard Me. And I know that You always hear Me, but because of the people who are standing by I said this, that they may believe that You sent Me." Now when He had said these things, He cried with a loud voice, "Lazarus, come forth!" And he who had died came out bound hand and foot with graveclothes, and his face was wrapped with a cloth. Jesus said to them, "Loose him, and let him go." (NKJV)

A. What does this Scripture tell me about what God thinks about this topic?
- God thinks…
- God is…
- God…

B. What does this Scripture tell me about people?
  - People are…
  - People need to…
  - People…

C. How do I apply this Scripture to my life today?
  - I will…

D. Write out a prayer asking the Holy Spirit to empower you with strength to live out what He taught you today.

Grace Note:

Jesus wept over the death of His friend. It's OK to cry. Loss and pain are real. Jesus identifies with your loss and grief. At the same time, Jesus is the resurrection and the life and He will make all things new! Stay close to Christ. Let Him love you through your pain. And know that as you walk with Jesus, you will see your loved ones again in heaven.

What does God think about...
DEATH?

1 Corinthians 15:1-57 Now I would remind you, brothers, of the gospel I preached to you, which you received, in which you stand, and by which you are being saved, if you hold fast to the word I preached to you—unless you believed in vain.

For I delivered to you as of first importance what I also received: that Christ died for our sins in accordance with the Scriptures, that he was buried, that he was raised on the third day in accordance with the Scriptures, and that he appeared to Cephas, then to the twelve. Then he appeared to more than five hundred brothers at one time, most of whom are still alive, though some have fallen asleep. Then he appeared to James, then to all the apostles. Last of all, as to one untimely born, he appeared also to me. For I am the least of the apostles, unworthy to be called an apostle, because I persecuted the church of God. But by the grace of God I am what I am, and his grace toward me was not in vain. On the contrary, I worked harder than any of them, though it was not I, but the grace of God that is with me. Whether then it was I or they, so we preach and so you believed.

Now if Christ is proclaimed as raised from the dead, how can some of you say that there is no resurrection of the dead? But if there is no resurrection of the dead, then not even Christ has been raised. And if Christ has not been raised, then our preaching is in vain and your faith is in vain. We are even found to be misrepresenting God, because we testified about God that he raised Christ, whom he did not raise if it is true that the dead are not raised. For if the dead are not raised, not even Christ has been raised. And if Christ has not been raised, your faith is futile and you are still in your sins. Then those also who have fallen asleep in Christ have perished. If in Christ we have hope in this life only, we are of all people most to be pitied.

But in fact Christ has been raised from the dead, the firstfruits of those who have fallen asleep. For as by a man came death, by a man has come also the resurrection of the dead. For as in Adam all die, so also in Christ shall all be made alive. But each in his own order: Christ the firstfruits, then at his coming those who belong to Christ. Then comes the end, when he delivers the kingdom to God the Father after destroying every rule and every authority and power. For he must reign until he has put all his enemies under his feet. The last enemy to be destroyed is death. For "God has put all things in subjection under his feet." But when it says, "all things are put in subjection," it is plain that he is excepted who put all things in subjection under him. When all things are subjected to him, then the Son himself will also be subjected to him who put all things in subjection under him, that God may be all in all.

Otherwise, what do people mean by being baptized on behalf of the dead? If the dead are not raised at all, why are people baptized on their behalf? Why are we in danger every hour? I protest, brothers, by my pride in you, which I have in Christ Jesus our Lord, I die every day! What do I gain if, humanly speaking, I fought with beasts at Ephesus? If the dead are not raised, "Let us eat and drink, for tomorrow we die." Do not be deceived: "Bad company ruins good morals." Wake up from your drunken stupor, as is right, and do not go on sinning. For some have no knowledge of God. I say this to your shame.

But someone will ask, "How are the dead raised? With what kind of body do they come?" You foolish person! What you sow does not come to life unless it dies. And what you sow is not the body that is to be, but a bare kernel, perhaps of wheat or of some other grain. But God gives it a body as he has chosen, and to each kind of seed its own body. For not all flesh is the same, but there is one kind for humans, another for animals, another for birds, and another for fish. There are heavenly bodies and earthly bodies, but the glory of the heavenly is of one kind, and the glory of the earthly is of another. There is one glory of the sun, and another glory of the moon, and another glory of the stars; for star differs from star in glory.

So is it with the resurrection of the dead. What is sown is perishable; what is raised is imperishable. It is sown in dishonor; it is raised in glory. It is sown in weakness; it is raised in power. It is sown a natural body; it is raised a spiritual body. If there is a natural body, there is also a spiritual body. Thus it is written, "The first man Adam became a living being"; the last Adam became a life-giving spirit. But it is not the spiritual that is first but the natural, and then the spiritual. The first man was from the earth, a man of dust; the second man is from heaven. As was the man of dust, so also are those who are of the dust, and as is the man of heaven, so also are those who are of heaven. Just as we have borne the image of the man of dust, we shall also bear the image of the man of heaven.

I tell you this, brothers: flesh and blood cannot inherit the kingdom of God, nor does the perishable inherit the imperishable. Behold! I tell you a mystery. We shall not all sleep, but we shall all be changed, in a moment, in the twinkling of an eye, at the last trumpet. For the trumpet will sound, and the dead will be raised imperishable, and we shall be changed. For this perishable body must put on the imperishable, and this mortal body must put on immortality. When the perishable puts on the imperishable, and the mortal puts on immortality, then shall come to pass the saying that is written:

"Death is swallowed up in victory. O death, where is your victory? O death, where is your sting?"

The sting of death is sin, and the power of sin is the law. But thanks be to God, who gives us the victory through our Lord Jesus Christ. (ESV)

A. What does this Scripture tell me about what God thinks about this topic?
    - God thinks…
    - God is…
    - God…

B. What does this Scripture tell me about people?
    - People are…
    - People need to…
    - People…

C. How do I apply this Scripture to my life today?
    - I will…

D. Write out a prayer asking the Holy Spirit to empower you with strength to live out what He taught you today.

Grace Note:
Death died when Jesus rose. All followers of Jesus that have died will rise again like He rose! His resurrection is a deposit guaranteeing our resurrection. So don't lose hope. Keep the faith. You will see those you love again if they walked with Jesus.

What does God think about...
DEPRESSION?

Psalm 42:1-11 *As the deer pants for streams of water, so my soul pants for you, my God. My soul thirsts for God, for the living God. When can I go and meet with God? My tears have been my food day and night, while people say to me all day long, "Where is your God?"*

These things I remember as I pour out my soul: how I used to go to the house of God under the protection of the Mighty One with shouts of joy and praise among the festive throng.

Why, my soul, are you downcast? Why so disturbed within me? Put your hope in God, for I will yet praise him, my Savior and my God.

My soul is downcast within me; therefore I will remember you from the land of the Jordan, the heights of Hermon—from Mount Mizar. Deep calls to deep in the roar of your waterfalls; all your waves and breakers have swept over me.

By day the LORD directs his love, at night his song is with me—a prayer to the God of my life. I say to God my Rock, "Why have you forgotten me? Why must I go about mourning, oppressed by the enemy?"

My bones suffer mortal agony as my foes taunt me, saying to me all day long, "Where is your God?"

Why, my soul, are you downcast? Why so disturbed within me? Put your hope in God, for I will yet praise him, my Savior and my God. (NIV)

A. What does this Scripture tell me about what God thinks about this topic?
   - God thinks...
   - God is...
   - God...

B. What does this Scripture tell me about people?
   - People are...
   - People need to...
   - People...

C. How do I apply this Scripture to my life today?
   - I will...

D. Write out a prayer asking the Holy Spirit to empower you with strength to live out what He taught you today.

Grace Note:
Everyone goes through seasons of discouragement. The Scriptures are clear that Christ can set you free from depression. However, sometimes

people have a chemical imbalance that can and should be treated medically. If you are dealing with severe depression, please go see a professional and let them guide you to a course of action to set you free from this debilitating disease.

What does God think about...
DISCIPLE MAKING?

Luke 10:1-20 *After these things the Lord appointed seventy others also, and sent them two by two before His face into every city and place where He Himself was about to go.*

Then He said to them, "The harvest truly is great, but the laborers are few; therefore pray the Lord of the harvest to send out laborers into His harvest. Go your way; behold, I send you out as lambs among wolves. Carry neither money bag, knapsack, nor sandals; and greet no one along the road. But whatever house you enter, first say, 'Peace to this house.' And if a son of peace is there, your peace will rest on it; if not, it will return to you. And remain in the same house, eating and drinking such things as they give, for the laborer is worthy of his wages. Do not go from house to house. Whatever city you enter, and they receive you, eat such things as are set before you. And heal the sick there, and say to them, 'The kingdom of God has come near to you.' But whatever city you enter, and they do not receive you, go out into its streets and say, 'The very dust of your city which clings to us we wipe off against you. Nevertheless know this, that the kingdom of God has come near you.' But I say to you that it will be more tolerable in that Day for Sodom than for that city.

"Woe to you, Chorazin! Woe to you, Bethsaida! For if the mighty works which were done in you had been done in Tyre and Sidon, they would have repented long ago, sitting in sackcloth and ashes. But it will be more tolerable for Tyre and Sidon at the judgment than for you. And you, Capernaum, who are exalted to heaven, will be brought down to Hades. He who hears you hears Me, he who

rejects you rejects Me, and he who rejects Me rejects Him who sent Me."

Then the seventy returned with joy, saying, "Lord, even the demons are subject to us in Your name."

And He said to them, "I saw Satan fall like lightning from heaven. Behold, I give you the authority to trample on serpents and scorpions, and over all the power of the enemy, and nothing shall by any means hurt you. Nevertheless do not rejoice in this, that the spirits are subject to you, but rather rejoice because your names are written in heaven." (NKJV)

A. What does this Scripture tell me about what God thinks about this topic?
- God thinks...
- God is...
- God...

B. What does this Scripture tell me about people?
- People are...
- People need to...
- People...

C. How do I apply this Scripture to my life today?
- I will...

D. Write out a prayer asking the Holy Spirit to empower you with strength to live out what He taught you today.

Grace Note:

Jesus left you on earth to make disciples of the people around you. Don't get discouraged if some seem uninterested. Remember this text, the disciples just went to the next town or looked for the next person rather than sitting in rejection. If those around you seem uninterested in the gospel, forgive them and love them, but then go find somebody else who is interested. There is a person of peace waiting to welcome you if you will keep searching for that person. God wants you to become a disciple maker. He wants to use your life to rescue somebody else from the kingdom of darkness.

What does God think about...

DIVORCE?

Matthew 5:27-32 *"You have heard that it was said, 'You shall not commit adultery.' But I say to you that everyone who looks at a woman with lustful intent has already committed adultery with her in his heart. If your right eye causes you to sin, tear it out and throw it away. For it is better that you lose one of your members than that your whole body be thrown into hell. And if your right hand causes you to sin, cut it off and throw it away. For it is better that you lose one of your members than that your whole body go into hell.*

It was also said, 'Whoever divorces his wife, let him give her a certificate of divorce.' But I say to you that everyone who divorces his wife, except on the ground of sexual immorality, makes her commit adultery, and whoever marries a divorced woman commits adultery." (ESV)

A. What does this Scripture tell me about what God thinks about this topic?
- God thinks...
- God is...
- God...

B. What does this Scripture tell me about people?
- People are...
- People need to...
- People...

C. How do I apply this Scripture to my life today?
- I will...

D. Write out a prayer asking the Holy Spirit to empower you with strength to live out what He taught you today.

Grace Note:
Jesus gives infidelity as an acceptable reason for divorce. But please, before you pull that trigger, go see a Christian marriage counselor together. Thousands of men and women have been through the pain of infidelity and Jesus has rescued their marriages and set them on a path of unity and love. Christ can overcome a dysfunctional marriage.

What does God think about...
THE END OF THE WORLD?

Matthew 24:3-44 *Later, Jesus sat on the Mount of Olives. His disciples came to him privately and said, "Tell us, when will all this happen? What sign will signal your return and the end of the world?"*

Jesus told them, "Don't let anyone mislead you, for many will come in my name, claiming, 'I am the Messiah. They will deceive many. And you will hear of wars and threats of wars, but don't panic. Yes, these things must take place, but the end won't follow immediately. Nation will go to war against nation, and kingdom against kingdom. There will be famines and earthquakes in many parts of the world. But all this is only the first of the birth pains, with more to come.

Then you will be arrested, persecuted, and killed. You will be hated all over the world because you are my followers. And many will turn away from me and betray and hate each other. And many false prophets will appear and will deceive many people. Sin will be rampant everywhere, and the love of many will grow cold. But the one who endures to the end will be saved.

And the Good News about the Kingdom will be preached throughout the whole world, so that all nations will hear it; and then the end will come. The day is coming when you will see what Daniel the prophet spoke about—the sacrilegious object that causes desecration standing in the Holy Place." (Reader, pay attention!)

"Then those in Judea must flee to the hills. A person out on the deck of a roof must not go down into the house to pack. A person out in the field must not return even to get a coat. How terrible it will be for pregnant women and for nursing mothers in those days. And pray that your flight will not be in winter or on the Sabbath. For there will be greater anguish than at any time since the world began. And it will never be so great again. In fact, unless that time of calamity is shortened, not a single person will survive. But it will be shortened for the sake of God's chosen ones.

Then if anyone tells you, 'Look, here is the Messiah,' or 'There he is,' don't believe it. For false messiahs and false prophets will rise up and perform great signs and wonders so as to deceive, if possible, even God's chosen ones. See, I have warned you about this ahead of time. So if someone tells you, 'Look, the Messiah is out in the desert,' don't bother to go and look. Or, 'Look, he is hiding here,' don't believe it! For as the lightning flashes in the east and shines to the west, so it will be when the Son of Man comes.

Just as the gathering of vultures shows there is a carcass nearby, so these signs indicate that the end is near. Immediately after the anguish of those days, the sun will be darkened, the moon will give no light, the stars will fall from the sky, and the powers in the heavens will be shaken.

And then at last, the sign that the Son of Man is coming will appear in the heavens, and there will be deep mourning among all the peoples of the earth. And they will see the Son of Man coming on the clouds of heaven with power and great glory. And he will send out his angels with the mighty blast of a trumpet, and they will gather his chosen ones from all over the world—from the farthest ends of the earth and heaven.

Now learn a lesson from the fig tree. When its branches bud and its leaves begin to sprout, you know that summer is near. In the same

way, when you see all these things, you can know his return is very near, right at the door. I tell you the truth, this generation will not pass from the scene until all these things take place. Heaven and earth will disappear, but my words will never disappear.
However, no one knows the day or hour when these things will happen, not even the angels in heaven or the Son himself. Only the Father knows.

When the Son of Man returns, it will be like it was in Noah's day. In those days before the flood, the people were enjoying banquets and parties and weddings right up to the time Noah entered his boat. People didn't realize what was going to happen until the flood came and swept them all away. That is the way it will be when the Son of Man comes.

Two men will be working together in the field; one will be taken, the other left. Two women will be grinding flour at the mill; one will be taken, the other left. So you, too, must keep watch! For you don' know what day your Lord is coming.

Understand this: If a homeowner knew exactly when a burglar was coming, he would keep watch and not permit his house to be broken into. You also must be ready all the time, for the Son of Man will come when least expected. (NLT)

A. What does this Scripture tell me about what God thinks about this topic?
- God thinks...
- God is...
- God...

B. What does this Scripture tell me about people?
- People are…
- People need to…
- People…

C. How do I apply this Scripture to my life today?
- I will…

D. Write out a prayer asking the Holy Spirit to empower you with strength to live out what He taught you today.

Grace Note:
Sometimes people say Jesus is not going to return, it's been too long. But I would say Jesus has not returned because He loves you and He is giving all of us a little more time to repent, to turn to Him and trust Him and follow Him. The reason He is not here yet is because He is patient with this world and wants everyone to come to repentance. So turn to Christ today before time is up. Give your heart to Christ today, don't wait any longer. He is going to return and change the world, and you want to be on the winning team.

What does God think about...
EVANGELISM?

Acts 8:26-40 Now an angel of the Lord said to Philip, "Go south to the road—the desert road—that goes down from Jerusalem to Gaza." So he started out, and on his way he met an Ethiopian eunuch, an important official in charge of all the treasury of the Kandake (which means "queen of the Ethiopians"). This man had gone to Jerusalem to worship, and on his way home was sitting in his chariot reading the Book of Isaiah the prophet. The Spirit told Philip, "Go to that chariot and stay near it."

Then Philip ran up to the chariot and heard the man reading Isaiah the prophet. "Do you understand what you are reading?"

Philip asked. "How can I," he said, "unless someone explains it to me?" So he invited Philip to come up and sit with him.

This is the passage of Scripture the eunuch was reading:

"He was led like a sheep to the slaughter, and as a lamb before its shearer is silent, so he did not open his mouth. In his humiliation he was deprived of justice. Who can speak of his descendants? For his life was taken from the earth."

The eunuch asked Philip, "Tell me, please, who is the prophet talking about, himself or someone else?" Then Philip began with that very passage of Scripture and told him the good news about Jesus.

As they traveled along the road, they came to some water and the eunuch said, "Look, here is water. What can stand in the way of my being baptized?" And he gave orders to stop the chariot. Then both Philip and the eunuch went down into the water and Philip baptized him. When they came up out of the water, the Spirit of the Lord suddenly took Philip away, and the eunuch did not see him again, but went on his way rejoicing. Philip, however, appeared at Azotus and traveled about, preaching the gospel in all the towns until he reached Caesarea. (NIV)

A. What does this Scripture tell me about what God thinks about this topic?
   ▪   God thinks…
   ▪   God is…
   ▪   God…

B. What does this Scripture tell me about people?
   ▪   People are…
   ▪   People need to…
   ▪   People…

C. How do I apply this Scripture to my life today?
   ▪   I will…

D. Write out a prayer asking the Holy Spirit to empower you with strength to live out what He taught you today.

Grace Note:

This text shows us that, directed by the Spirit of God, we can lead people to the Savior if we look for opportunities. My prayer for you is that you look for opportunities wherever you go, and you open your mouth like Phillip did and point people to Jesus. One of the great privileges of your life is to be able to baptize somebody that you lead to Christ! God's got this destiny for you! So open your eyes and follow the leading of the Spirit. Open your mouth and let Him lead you to people you can help cross the line of faith and follow Jesus.

What does God think about...
EVOLUTION?

Genesis 1:1-2:4 *In the beginning, God created the heavens and the earth. The earth was without form and void, and darkness was over the face of the deep. And the Spirit of God was hovering over the face of the waters.*

And God said, "Let there be light," and there was light. And God saw that the light was good. And God separated the light from the darkness. God called the light Day, and the darkness he called Night. And there was evening and there was morning, the first day.

And God said, "Let there be an expanse in the midst of the waters, and let it separate the waters from the waters." And God made the expanse and separated the waters that were under the expanse from the waters that were above the expanse. And it was so. And God called the expanse Heaven. And there was evening and there was morning, the second day.

And God said, "Let the waters under the heavens be gathered together into one place, and let the dry land appear." And it was so. God called the dry land Earth, and the waters that were gathered together he called Seas. And God saw that it was good.

And God said, "Let the earth sprout vegetation, plants yielding seed, and fruit trees bearing fruit in which is their seed, each according to its kind, on the earth." And it was so. The earth brought forth vegetation, plants yielding seed according to their own kinds, and trees bearing fruit in which is their seed, each according to its kind. And God saw that it was good. And there was evening and there was morning, the third day.

And God said, "Let there be lights in the expanse of the heavens to separate the day from the night. And let them be for signs and for seasons, and for days and years, and let them be lights in the expanse of the heavens to give light upon the earth." And it was so. And God made the two great lights—the greater light to rule the day and the lesser light to rule the night—and the stars. And God set them in the expanse of the heavens to give light on the earth, to rule over the day and over the night, and to separate the light from the darkness. And God saw that it was good. And there was evening and there was morning, the fourth day.

And God said, "Let the waters swarm with swarms of living creatures, and let birds fly above the earth across the expanse of the heavens." So God created the great sea creatures and every living creature that moves, with which the waters swarm, according to their kinds, and every winged bird according to its kind. And God saw that it was good. And God blessed them, saying, "Be fruitful and multiply and fill the waters in the seas, and let birds multiply on the earth." And there was evening and there was morning, the fifth day.

And God said, "Let the earth bring forth living creatures according to their kinds—livestock and creeping things and beasts of the earth according to their kinds." And it was so. And God made the beasts of the earth according to their kinds and the livestock according to their kinds, and everything that creeps on the ground according to its kind. And God saw that it was good.

Then God said, "Let us make man in our image, after our likeness. And let them have dominion over the fish of the sea and over the birds of the heavens and over the livestock and over all the earth and over every creeping thing that creeps on the earth."

So God created man in his own image, in the image of God he created him; male and female he created them.

And God blessed them. And God said to them, "Be fruitful and multiply and fill the earth and subdue it, and have dominion over the fish of the sea and over the birds of the heavens and over every living thing that moves on the earth." And God said, "Behold, I have given you every plant yielding seed that is on the face of all the earth, and every tree with seed in its fruit. You shall have them for food. And to every beast of the earth and to every bird of the heavens and to everything that creeps on the earth, everything that has the breath of life, I have given every green plant for food." And it was so. And God saw everything that he had made, and behold, it was very good. And there was evening and there was morning, the sixth day.

Thus the heavens and the earth were finished, and all the host of them. And on the seventh day God finished his work that he had done, and he rested on the seventh day from all his work that he had done. So God blessed the seventh day and made it holy, because on it God rested from all his work that he had done in creation.

These are the generations of the heavens and the earth when they were created, in the day that the LORD God made the earth and the heavens. (ESV)

A. What does this Scripture tell me about what God thinks about this topic?
- God thinks…
- God is…
- God…

B. What does this Scripture tell me about people?
  - People are…
  - People need to…
  - People…

C. How do I apply this Scripture to my life today?
  - I will…

D. Write out a prayer asking the Holy Spirit to empower you with strength to live out what He taught you today.

Grace Note:

Genesis chapter one seems pretty clear that God created the universe. This is important. A loving God created this world, and you, with purpose and dignity. You are made in His image and are not an accident of nature. He wants to commune with you and love you and walk with you. You are important to Him, and He built this world for you to enjoy. So seek Him because He's waiting to talk to you. Follow Him because He loves you.

What does God think about...
FATHERHOOD?

Ephesians 6:1-4 *Children, obey your parents in the Lord, for this is right. "Honor your father and mother," which is the first commandment with promise: "that it may be well with you and you may live long on the earth."*

And you, fathers, do not provoke your children to wrath, but bring them up in the training and admonition of the Lord. (NKJV)

Deuteronomy 6:1-7 *"These are the commands, decrees, and regulations that the Lord your God commanded me to teach you. You must obey them in the land you are about to enter and occupy, and you and your children and grandchildren must fear the Lord your God as long as you live.*

If you obey all his decrees and commands, you will enjoy a long life. Listen closely, Israel, and be careful to obey. Then all will go well with you, and you will have many children in the land flowing with milk and honey, just as the Lord, the God of your ancestors, promised you.

Listen, O Israel! The Lord is our God, the Lord alone.

And you must love the Lord your God with all your heart, all your soul, and all your strength. And you must commit yourselves wholeheartedly to these commands that I am giving you today.

Repeat them again and again to your children. Talk about them when you are at home and when you are on the road, when you are going to bed and when you are getting up." (NLT)

A. What does this Scripture tell me about what God thinks about this topic?
   - God thinks...
   - God is...
   - God...

B. What does this Scripture tell me about people?
   - People are...
   - People need to...
   - People...

C. How do I apply this Scripture to my life today?
   - I will...

D. Write out a prayer asking the Holy Spirit to empower you with strength to live out what He taught you today.

Grace Note:
The best manual for raising kids is the Scriptures. God is a good Father, so He knows best how to be a good dad. So lean into His words here, and

raise your kids to walk with God. Make this the priority of your parenting and your kids will succeed in this world.

What does God think about...
FINANCIAL BLESSING?

Malachi 3:8-12 *"Will a mere mortal rob God? Yet you rob me.*

But you ask, 'How are we robbing you?'

In tithes and offerings. You are under a curse—your whole nation—because you are robbing me.

Bring the whole tithe into the storehouse, that there may be food in my house. Test me in this," says the LORD Almighty, "and see if I will not throw open the floodgates of heaven and pour out so much blessing that there will not be room enough to store it.

I will prevent pests from devouring your crops, and the vines in your fields will not drop their fruit before it is ripe," says the LORD Almighty. Then all the nations will call you blessed, for yours will be a delightful land," says the LORD Almighty. (NIV)

A. What does this Scripture tell me about what God thinks about this topic?
- God thinks…
- God is…
- God…

B. What does this Scripture tell me about people?
- People are…
- People need to…
- People…

C. How do I apply this Scripture to my life today?
- I will…

D. Write out a prayer asking the Holy Spirit to empower you with strength to live out what He taught you today.

Grace Note:
Notice that the heart of this text is to bless you. God wants to pour out abundant blessing on your life financially. Honor Him with your wealth and with all of your income. When you do this, God promises to pour out blessings on you and your family. I don't know what those blessings specifically will be, but I do know He blesses your life when you honor Him with your income.

What does God think about...
FRIENDSHIPS?

Ecclesiastes 4:9-12 *Two are better than one, because they have a good reward for their labor. For if they fall, one will lift up his companion. But woe to him who is alone when he falls, for he has no one to help him up.*

Again, if two lie down together, they will keep warm; but how can one be warm alone? Though one may be overpowered by another, two can withstand him. And a threefold cord is not quickly broken. (NKJV)

Proverbs 12:26 *The righteous choose their friends carefully, but the way of the wicked leads them astray. (NIV)*

A. What does this Scripture tell me about what God thinks about this topic?
- God thinks…
- God is…
- God…

B. What does this Scripture tell me about people?
- People are…
- People need to…
- People…

C. How do I apply this Scripture to my life today?

- I will…

D. Write out a prayer asking the Holy Spirit to empower you with strength to live out what He taught you today.

Grace Note:
We need each other. Christianity is a team sport. We need fellowship and encouragement and love from other Christians. We need their wisdom and guidance. We need their prayers and support. We need their time and attention. This is one reason why church matters. As you go to church, find somebody to connect with as close as a brother or sister. Making a friend with someone at church who is spiritually wise and loves Jesus will get you through dark times in life and help you keep the faith.

What does God think about...
GOVERNMENT?

Romans 13:1-7 *Everyone must submit to governing authorities.*

For all authority comes from God, and those in positions of authority have been placed there by God. So anyone who rebels against authority is rebelling against what God has instituted, and they will be punished.

For the authorities do not strike fear in people who are doing right, but in those who are doing wrong.

Would you like to live without fear of the authorities? Do what is right, and they will honor you. The authorities are God's servants, sent for your good. But if you are doing wrong, of course you should be afraid, for they have the power to punish you.

They are God's servants, sent for the very purpose of punishing those who do what is wrong.

So you must submit to them, not only to avoid punishment, but also to keep a clear conscience.

Pay your taxes, too, for these same reasons. For government workers need to be paid. They are serving God in what they do.

Give to everyone what you owe them: Pay your taxes and government fees to those who collect them, and give respect and honor to those who are in authority. (NLT)

A. What does this Scripture tell me about what God thinks about this topic?
- God thinks...
- God is...
- God...

B. What does this Scripture tell me about people?
- People are...
- People need to...
- People...

C. How do I apply this Scripture to my life today?
- I will...

D. Write out a prayer asking the Holy Spirit to empower you with strength to live out what He taught you today.

Grace Note:
It's tough to treat those in the government with honor when they are sometimes dishonorable. The government in Paul's day was very dishonorable towards Christians. They were torturing and killing Christians as Paul wrote this text. So as difficult as it is to submit to and honor authority, please make the heart of your life respectful, submissive, honorable, and gracious towards those who lead us. Each of us will have

to pray about what that means specifically, but don't give up and get angry and rebellious. Rather, work to make this country a healthy, safe place to live in for all people.

What does God think about...
GUIDANCE - FINDING GOD'S PLAN?

Proverbs 3:1-8 *My son, do not forget my law, but let your heart keep my commands; for length of days and long life and peace they will add to you.*

Let not mercy and truth forsake you; bind them around your neck, write them on the tablet of your heart, and so find favor and high esteem in the sight of God and man.

Trust in the LORD with all your heart, and lean not on your own understanding; in all your ways acknowledge Him, and He shall direct your paths.

Do not be wise in your own eyes; fear the LORD and depart from evil. It will be health to your flesh, and strength to your bones. (NKJV)

A. What does this Scripture tell me about what God thinks about this topic?
- God thinks...
- God is...
- God...

B. What does this Scripture tell me about people?
- People are…
- People need to…
- People…

C. How do I apply this Scripture to my life today?
- I will…

D. Write out a prayer asking the Holy Spirit to empower you with strength to live out what He taught you today.

Grace Note:

The Spirit of God wants to guide your steps. Your decisions are important to God. So seek Him and trust Him. Reject your own understanding and lean on Christ for the direction of your life - He will never let you down.

What does God think about...
HANDLING DISAPPOINTMENT?

Psalm 46:1-11 *God is our refuge and strength, a very present help in trouble.*

Therefore we will not fear though the earth gives way, though the mountains be moved into the heart of the sea, though its waters roar and foam, though the mountains tremble at its swelling.

There is a river whose streams make glad the city of God, the holy habitation of the Most High. God is in the midst of her; she shall not be moved; God will help her when morning dawns.

The nations rage, the kingdoms totter; he utters his voice, the earth melts. The LORD of hosts is with us; the God of Jacob is our fortress.

Come, behold the works of the LORD, how he has brought desolations on the earth. He makes wars cease to the end of the earth; he breaks the bow and shatters the spear; he burns the chariots with fire.

"Be still, and know that I am God. I will be exalted among the nations, I will be exalted in the earth!"

The LORD of hosts is with us; the God of Jacob is our fortress. (ESV)

A. What does this Scripture tell me about what God thinks about this topic?
- God thinks...
- God is...
- God...

B. What does this Scripture tell me about people?
- People are...
- People need to...
- People...

C. How do I apply this Scripture to my life today?
- I will...

D. Write out a prayer asking the Holy Spirit to empower you with strength to live out what He taught you today.

Grace Note:
Many times life does not turn out how we planned or hoped it would go. Leaning into God as refuge and strength in moments of confusion and disappointment is the only way to make it through. Remember, He is not surprised or freaked out when things don't go your way! He knows it all and He knows how to redeem every disappointment and pain! So trust Him! Lean on Him! He is our help in our time of trouble.

What does God think about...
A HEALTHY MIND?

Philippians 4:4-9 *Always be full of joy in the Lord. I say it again—rejoice! Let everyone see that you are considerate in all you do. Remember, the Lord is coming soon.*

Don't worry about anything; instead, pray about everything.

Tell God what you need, and thank him for all he has done. Then you will experience God's peace, which exceeds anything we can understand. His peace will guard your hearts and minds as you live in Christ Jesus.

And now, dear brothers and sisters, one final thing. Fix your thoughts on what is true, and honorable, and right, and pure, and lovely, and admirable.

Think about things that are excellent and worthy of praise.

Keep putting into practice all you learned and received from me—everything you heard from me and saw me doing. Then the God of peace will be with you. (NLT)

A. What does this Scripture tell me about what God thinks about this topic?
- God thinks...
- God is...
- God...

B. What does this Scripture tell me about people?
- People are…
- People need to…
- People…

C. How do I apply this Scripture to my life today?
- I will…

D. Write out a prayer asking the Holy Spirit to empower you with strength to live out what He taught you today.

Grace Note:
Where the mind goes, the man follows. Remember, what you think about, you bring about. Thoughts are like trains, they always take you to a destination. So if you focus on negativity, your life moves in a negative direction. Focus on positive things and your life moves in a positive direction. You cannot have a positive life and a negative mind. So reject negativity and things that are unwholesome. Focus on things that are beautiful and lovely and worthy of praise! Focus on healthy things so your life stays healthy!

What does God think about...
HEARING GOD'S VOICE?

John 10:1-16, 26-30 "Very truly I tell you Pharisees, anyone who does not enter the sheep pen by the gate, but climbs in by some other way, is a thief and a robber. The one who enters by the gate is the shepherd of the sheep. The gatekeeper opens the gate for him, and the sheep listen to his voice. He calls his own sheep by name and leads them out. When he has brought out all his own, he goes on ahead of them, and his sheep follow him because they know his voice. But they will never follow a stranger; in fact, they will run away from him because they do not recognize a stranger's voice." Jesus used this figure of speech, but the Pharisees did not understand what he was telling them.

Therefore Jesus said again, "Very truly I tell you, I am the gate for the sheep. All who have come before me are thieves and robbers, but the sheep have not listened to them. I am the gate; whoever enters through me will be saved. They will come in and go out, and find pasture. The thief comes only to steal and kill and destroy; I have come that they may have life, and have it to the full.
"I am the good shepherd. The good shepherd lays down his life for the sheep. The hired hand is not the shepherd and does not own the sheep. So when he sees the wolf coming, he abandons the sheep and runs away. Then the wolf attacks the flock and scatters it. The man runs away because he is a hired hand and cares nothing for the sheep.

"I am the good shepherd; I know my sheep and my sheep know me—just as the Father knows me and I know the Father—and I lay down my life for the sheep. I have other sheep that are not of this sheep pen. I must bring them also. They too will listen to my voice, and there shall be one flock and one shepherd.

"…but you do not believe because you are not my sheep. My sheep listen to my voice; I know them, and they follow me. I give them eternal life, and they shall never perish; no one will snatch them out of my hand. My Father, who has given them to me, is greater than all; no one can snatch them out of my Father's hand. I and the Father are one." (NIV)

A. What does this Scripture tell me about what God thinks about this topic?
- God thinks…
- God is…
- God…

B. What does this Scripture tell me about people?
- People are…
- People need to…
- People…

C. How do I apply this Scripture to my life today?
- I will…

D. Write out a prayer asking the Holy Spirit to empower you with strength to live out what He taught you today.

Grace Note:

Jesus is speaking to you! This text says those that are His followers hear His voice and respond to Him! If you have never heard the voice of God, spend the next 30 days asking for Jesus to speak to you every day. He will talk to you if you will listen.

What does God think about...
HEAVEN AND HELL?

Luke 16:19-31 *There was a rich man who was clothed in purple and fine linen and who feasted sumptuously every day. And at his gate was laid a poor man named Lazarus, covered with sores, who desired to be fed with what fell from the rich man's table. Moreover, even the dogs came and licked his sores. The poor man died and was carried by the angels to Abraham's side. The rich man also died and was buried, and in Hades, being in torment, he lifted up his eyes and saw Abraham far off and Lazarus at his side.*

And he called out, "Father Abraham, have mercy on me, and send Lazarus to dip the end of his finger in water and cool my tongue, for I am in anguish in this flame."

But Abraham said, "Child, remember that you in your lifetime received your good things, and Lazarus in like manner bad things; but now he is comforted here, and you are in anguish. And besides all this, between us and you a great chasm has been fixed, in order that those who would pass from here to you may not be able, and none may cross from there to us."

And he said, "Then I beg you, father, to send him to my father's house—for I have five brothers—so that he may warn them, lest they also come into this place of torment."

But Abraham said, "They have Moses and the Prophets; let them hear them." And he said, "No, father Abraham, but if someone goes to them from the dead, they will repent." He said to him, "If they do not hear Moses and the Prophets, neither will they be convinced if someone should rise from the dead." (ESV)

A. What does this Scripture tell me about what God thinks about this topic?
- God thinks…
- God is…
- God…

B. What does this Scripture tell me about people?
- People are…
- People need to…
- People…

C. How do I apply this Scripture to my life today?
- I will…

D. Write out a prayer asking the Holy Spirit to empower you with strength to live out what He taught you today.

Grace Note:
We will each spend eternity in one of two places: heaven or hell. This text is so clear on what happens to people when they die. There's no waiting around. There are no second chances. Decide now in this life to walk with Jesus so you enjoy paradise with Him forever!

What does God think about...
THE HOLY SPIRIT?

John 16:5-15 *But now I go away to Him who sent Me, and none of you asks Me, "Where are You going?" But because I have said these things to you, sorrow has filled your heart.*

Nevertheless I tell you the truth. It is to your advantage that I go away; for if I do not go away, the Helper will not come to you; but if I depart, I will send Him to you.

And when He has come, He will convict the world of sin, and of righteousness, and of judgment: of sin, because they do not believe in Me; of righteousness, because I go to My Father and you see Me no more; of judgment, because the ruler of this world is judged. I still have many things to say to you, but you cannot bear them now.

However, when He, the Spirit of truth, has come, He will guide you into all truth; for He will not speak on His own authority, but whatever He hears He will speak; and He will tell you things to come.

He will glorify Me, for He will take of what is Mine and declare it to you. All things that the Father has are Mine. Therefore I said that He will take of Mine and declare it to you. (NKJV)

A. What does this Scripture tell me about what God thinks about this topic?
- God thinks...
- God is...
- God...

B. What does this Scripture tell me about people?
  - People are…
  - People need to…
  - People…

C. How do I apply this Scripture to my life today?
  - I will…

D. Write out a prayer asking the Holy Spirit to empower you with strength to live out what He taught you today.

Grace Note:
Jesus had to leave so the Holy Spirit could live in you. One of the members of the Trinity resides inside of you as a believer! So you have all the power, and all the wisdom, and all the guidance you need to make it in life. Trust in the Spirit of God's direction. Lean in to the Holy Spirit. He will never direct you away from the Word of God, but will always point to what the Scriptures teach. You're going to be OK because you have the Holy Spirit guiding your life!

What does God think about...
HOMOSEXUALITY?

Romans 1:18-31 *God shows his anger from heaven against all sinful, wicked people who suppress the truth by their wickedness. They know the truth about God because he has made it obvious to them.*

For ever since the world was created, people have seen the earth and sky. Through everything God made, they can clearly see his invisible qualities—his eternal power and divine nature. So they have no excuse for not knowing God.

Yes, they knew God, but they wouldn't worship him as God or even give him thanks. And they began to think up foolish ideas of what God was like. As a result, their minds became dark and confused. Claiming to be wise, they instead became utter fools.

And instead of worshiping the glorious, ever-living God, they worshiped idols made to look like mere people and birds and animals and reptiles.

So God abandoned them to do whatever shameful things their hearts desired. As a result, they did vile and degrading things with each other's bodies. They traded the truth about God for a lie. So they worshiped and served the things God created instead of the Creator himself, who is worthy of eternal praise! Amen.

That is why God abandoned them to their shameful desires. Even the women turned against the natural way to have sex and instead indulged in sex with each other. And the men, instead of having normal sexual relations with women, burned with lust for each other. Men did shameful things with other men, and as a result of this sin, they suffered within themselves the penalty they deserved.

Since they thought it foolish to acknowledge God, he abandoned them to their foolish thinking and let them do things that should never be done. Their lives became full of every kind of wickedness, sin, greed, hate, envy, murder, quarreling, deception, malicious behavior, and gossip. They are backstabbers, haters of God, insolent, proud, and boastful. They invent new ways of sinning, and they disobey their parents. They refuse to understand, break their promises, are heartless, and have no mercy. (NLT)

A. What does this Scripture tell me about what God thinks about this topic?
  - God thinks…
  - God is…
  - God…

B. What does this Scripture tell me about people?
  - People are…
  - People need to…
  - People…

C. How do I apply this Scripture to my life today?
  - I will…

D. Write out a prayer asking the Holy Spirit to empower you with strength to live out what He taught you today.

Grace Note:

This text is pretty specific. Homosexual behavior is sexual misconduct and is against the will of God. However, Jesus loves and died for people who struggle with homosexual feelings. Know that the grace of God covers all sin - including this one! When we turn to Christ, He can set us free of desires that are not from heaven. As we walk with Him, He can change the innermost places of our hearts and set us on a path toward freedom.

What does God think about...
JESUS?

John 1:1-18 In the beginning was the Word, and the Word was with God, and the Word was God. He was in the beginning with God. All things were made through him, and without him was not any thing made that was made. In him was life, and the life was the light of men. The light shines in the darkness, and the darkness has not overcome it.

There was a man sent from God, whose name was John. He came as a witness, to bear witness about the light, that all might believe through him. He was not the light, but came to bear witness about the light.

The true light, which gives light to everyone, was coming into the world. He was in the world, and the world was made through him, yet the world did not know him. He came to his own, and his own people did not receive him. But to all who did receive him, who believed in his name, he gave the right to become children of God, who were born, not of blood nor of the will of the flesh nor of the will of man, but of God.

And the Word became flesh and dwelt among us, and we have seen his glory, glory as of the only Son from the Father, full of grace and truth. (John bore witness about him, and cried out, "This was he of whom I said, 'He who comes after me ranks before me, because he was before me.'") For from his fullness we have all received, grace upon grace. For the law was given through Moses; grace and truth came through Jesus Christ. No one has ever seen God; the only God, who is at the Father's side, he has made him known. (ESV)

A. What does this Scripture tell me about what God thinks about this topic?
   - God thinks...
   - God is...
   - God...

B. What does this Scripture tell me about people?
   - People are...
   - People need to...
   - People...

C. How do I apply this Scripture to my life today?
   - I will...

D. Write out a prayer asking the Holy Spirit to empower you with strength to live out what He taught you today.

Grace Note:
The Scriptures teach that Jesus is grace. This text says every blessing is from His grace! There is no other way to heaven. There's no other Savior. There's no other Creator. There is no other Lord. There is no other God! There is no way to be saved except through Christ. So, verbally confess with your mouth that Jesus is Lord! Commit right now to give your life to Him and let Him take you to greater things.

What does God think about...
MARRIAGE?

Ephesians 5:21-33 *Submit to one another out of reverence for Christ.*

Wives, submit yourselves to your own husbands as you do to the Lord. For the husband is the head of the wife as Christ is the head of the church, his body, of which he is the Savior. Now as the church submits to Christ, so also wives should submit to their husbands in everything.

Husbands, love your wives, just as Christ loved the church and gave himself up for her to make her holy, cleansing her by the washing with water through the word, and to present her to himself as a radiant church, without stain or wrinkle or any other blemish, but holy and blameless. In this same way, husbands ought to love their wives as their own bodies. He who loves his wife loves himself. After all, no one ever hated their own body, but they feed and care for their body, just as Christ does the church—for we are members of his body. "For this reason a man will leave his father and mother and be united to his wife, and the two will become one flesh." This is a profound mystery—but I am talking about Christ and the church. However, each one of you also must love his wife as he loves himself, and the wife must respect her husband. (NIV)

A. What does this Scripture tell me about what God thinks about this topic?
- God thinks...
- God is...
- God...

B. What does this Scripture tell me about people?
- People are...
- People need to...
- People...

C. How do I apply this Scripture to my life today?
- I will...

D. Write out a prayer asking the Holy Spirit to empower you with strength to live out what He taught you today.

Grace Note:
Notice here that marriage starts with mutual submission. The wife submits to the husband, and a husband gives up his selfish desires and self-sacrifices for the wife. This is what makes marriage beautiful. Each gives up their rights and loves the other unconditionally, selflessly, and with the goal of pleasing their spouse. This is Christian marriage, and this pleases Jesus.

What does God think about...
MONEY AND WEALTH?

Deuteronomy 8:11-18 *Beware that you do not forget the LORD your God by not keeping His commandments, His judgments, and His statutes which I command you today, lest—when you have eaten and are full, and have built beautiful houses and dwell in them; and when your herds and your flocks multiply, and your silver and your gold are multiplied, and all that you have is multiplied; when your heart is lifted up, and you forget the LORD your God who brought you out of the land of Egypt, from the house of bondage; who led you through that great and terrible wilderness, in which were fiery serpents and scorpions and thirsty land where there was no water; who brought water for you out of the flinty rock; who fed you in the wilderness with manna, which your fathers did not know, that He might humble you and that He might test you, to do you good in the end—then you say in your heart, "My power and the might of my hand have gained me this wealth."*

And you shall remember the LORD your God, for it is He who gives you power to get wealth, that He may establish His covenant which He swore to your fathers, as it is this day. (NKJV)

1 Timothy 6:17-19 *As for the rich in this present age, charge them not to be haughty, nor to set their hopes on the uncertainty of riches, but on God, who richly provides us with everything to enjoy. They are to do good, to be rich in good works, to be generous and ready to share, thus storing up treasure for themselves as a good foundation for the future, so that they may take hold of that which is truly life. (ESV)*

A. What does this Scripture tell me about what God thinks about this topic?
- God thinks…
- God is…
- God…

B. What does this Scripture tell me about people?
- People are…
- People need to…
- People…

C. How do I apply this Scripture to my life today?
- I will…

D. Write out a prayer asking the Holy Spirit to empower you with strength to live out what He taught you today.

Grace Note:
This text is amazing because it shows that God is the One that gives us the ability to make wealth! It is He who makes us wealthy and prosperous, so we honor Him with what we have. We remind ourselves it is all from Him. We use our money to do good and bless others and advance His Kingdom. I believe the more we honor Him with our wealth, the more God blesses our lives!

What does God think about...
MOTHERHOOD?

1 Samuel 1:1-28 There was a man named Elkanah who lived in Ramah in the region of Zuph in the hill country of Ephraim. He was the son of Jeroham, son of Elihu, son of Tohu, son of Zuph, of Ephraim. Elkanah had two wives, Hannah and Peninnah. Peninnah had children, but Hannah did not.

Each year Elkanah would travel to Shiloh to worship and sacrifice to the Lord of Heaven's Armies at the Tabernacle. The priests of the Lord at that time were the two sons of Eli—Hophni and Phinehas. On the days Elkanah presented his sacrifice, he would give portions of the meat to Peninnah and each of her children. And though he loved Hannah, he would give her only one choice portion because the Lord had given her no children. So Peninnah would taunt Hannah and make fun of her because the Lord had kept her from having children.

Year after year it was the same—Peninnah would taunt Hannah as they went to the Tabernacle. Each time, Hannah would be reduced to tears and would not even eat. "Why are you crying, Hannah?" Elkanah would ask. "Why aren't you eating? Why be downhearted just because you have no children? You have me—isn't that better than having ten sons?"

Once after a sacrificial meal at Shiloh, Hannah got up and went to pray. Eli the priest was sitting at his customary place beside the entrance of the Tabernacle. Hannah was in deep anguish, crying bitterly as she prayed to the Lord. And she made this vow: "O Lord of Heaven's Armies, if you will look upon my sorrow and answer my prayer and give me a son, then I will give him back to you. He will be yours for his entire lifetime, and as a sign that he has been dedicated to the Lord, his hair will never be cut." As she was praying to the Lord, Eli watched her. Seeing her lips moving but hearing no sound, he thought she had been drinking. "Must you come here drunk?" he demanded. "Throw away your wine!" "Oh no, sir!" she replied. "I haven't been drinking wine or anything stronger. But I am very discouraged, and I was pouring out my heart to the Lord. Don't think I am a wicked woman! For I have been praying out of great anguish and sorrow." "In that case," Eli said, "go in peace! May the God of Israel grant the request you have asked of him." "Oh, thank you, sir!" she exclaimed. Then she went back and began to eat again, and she was no longer sad. The entire family got up early the next morning and went to worship the Lord once more. Then they returned home to Ramah.

When Elkanah slept with Hannah, the Lord remembered her plea, and in due time she gave birth to a son. She named him Samuel, for she said, "I asked the Lord for him." The next year Elkanah and his family went on their annual trip to offer a sacrifice to the Lord and to keep his vow. But Hannah did not go. She told her husband, "Wait until the boy is weaned. Then I will take him to the Tabernacle and leave him there with the Lord permanently." "Whatever you think is best," Elkanah agreed. "Stay here for now, and may the Lord help you keep your promise." So she stayed home and nursed the boy until he was weaned.

When the child was weaned, Hannah took him to the Tabernacle in Shiloh. They brought along a three-year-old bull for the sacrifice and a basket of flour and some wine. After sacrificing the bull, they brought the boy to Eli. "Sir, do you remember me?" Hannah asked. "I am the very woman who stood here several years ago praying to the Lord. I asked the Lord to give me this boy, and he has granted my request. Now I am giving him to the Lord, and he will belong to the Lord his whole life." And they worshiped the Lord there. (NLT)

A. What does this Scripture tell me about what God thinks about this topic?
  - God thinks...
  - God is...
  - God...

B. What does this Scripture tell me about people?
  - People are...
  - People need to...
  - People...

C. How do I apply this Scripture to my life today?
  - I will...

D. Write out a prayer asking the Holy Spirit to empower you with strength to live out what He taught you today.

Grace Note:
This text is beautiful because this woman wants a child. When God blesses her with her son, she gives this son back to God out of gratitude for this blessing. What a powerful example of what a mother's purpose is! We thank God for our children and then we give them back to God for His purpose! We point our children in the direction of the Savior, and this is how we best steward our responsibility as parents.

What does God think about...
OTHER RELIGIONS?

1 Timothy 4:1-2 *The Spirit clearly says that in later times some will abandon the faith and follow deceiving spirits and things taught by demons. Such teachings come through hypocritical liars, whose consciences have been seared as with a hot iron. (NIV)*

I Corinthians 10:20 *...what pagans sacrifice they offer to demons and not to God. I do not want you to be participants with demons. (ESV)*

Exodus 20:3-6 *"You shall have no other gods before Me. You shall not make for yourself a carved image—any likeness of anything that is in heaven above, or that is in the earth beneath, or that is in the water under the earth; you shall not bow down to them nor serve them. For I, the LORD your God, am a jealous God, visiting the iniquity of the fathers upon the children to the third and fourth generations of those who hate Me, but showing mercy to thousands, to those who love Me and keep My commandments. (NKJV)*

A. What does this Scripture tell me about what God thinks about this topic?
    - God thinks...
    - God is...
    - God...

B. What does this Scripture tell me about people?
- People are...
- People need to...
- People...

C. How do I apply this Scripture to my life today?
- I will...

D. Write out a prayer asking the Holy Spirit to empower you with strength to live out what He taught you today.

Grace Note:

Let's be clear: other religions are doctrines of demons. There is only one way to heaven, and it is through Christ. Jesus is the only way, and we are to have no other gods but Him! To be Christian means not only to accept Christ, but to reject all other religions as false. There are not multiple ways to the Father, there is only Jesus.

What does God think about...
OVERCOMING HARDSHIP?

Job 1:1-2:10 *In the land of Uz there lived a man whose name was Job. This man was blameless and upright; he feared God and shunned evil. He had seven sons and three daughters, and he owned seven thousand sheep, three thousand camels, five hundred yoke of oxen and five hundred donkeys, and had a large number of servants. He was the greatest man among all the people of the East.*

His sons used to hold feasts in their homes on their birthdays, and they would invite their three sisters to eat and drink with them. When a period of feasting had run its course, Job would make arrangements for them to be purified. Early in the morning he would sacrifice a burnt offering for each of them, thinking, "Perhaps my children have sinned and cursed God in their hearts." This was Job's regular custom.

One day the angels came to present themselves before the LORD, and Satan also came with them. The LORD said to Satan, "Where have you come from?"

Satan answered the LORD, "From roaming throughout the earth, going back and forth on it."

Then the LORD said to Satan, "Have you considered my servant Job? There is no one on earth like him; he is blameless and upright, a man who fears God and shuns evil."

"Does Job fear God for nothing?" Satan replied. "Have you not put a hedge around him and his household and everything he has? You have blessed the work of his hands, so that his flocks and herds are spread throughout the land. But now stretch out your hand and strike everything he has, and he will surely curse you to your face."

The LORD said to Satan, "Very well, then, everything he has is in your power, but on the man himself do not lay a finger."

Then Satan went out from the presence of the LORD.

One day when Job's sons and daughters were feasting and drinking wine at the oldest brother's house, a messenger came to Job and said, "The oxen were plowing and the donkeys were grazing nearby, and the Sabeans attacked and made off with them. They put the servants to the sword, and I am the only one who has escaped to tell you!"

While he was still speaking, another messenger came and said, "The fire of God fell from the heavens and burned up the sheep and the servants, and I am the only one who has escaped to tell you!"

While he was still speaking, another messenger came and said, "The Chaldeans formed three raiding parties and swept down on your camels and made off with them. They put the servants to the sword, and I am the only one who has escaped to tell you!"

While he was still speaking, yet another messenger came and said, "Your sons and daughters were feasting and drinking wine at the oldest brother's house, when suddenly a mighty wind swept in from the desert and struck the four corners of the house. It collapsed on them and they are dead, and I am the only one who has escaped to tell you!"

At this, Job got up and tore his robe and shaved his head. Then he fell to the ground in worship and said: "Naked I came from my mother's womb, and naked I will depart. The LORD gave and the LORD has taken away; may the name of the LORD be praised."

In all this, Job did not sin by charging God with wrongdoing.

On another day the angels came to present themselves before the LORD, and Satan also came with them to present himself before him. And the LORD said to Satan, "Where have you come from?" Satan answered the LORD, "From roaming throughout the earth, going back and forth on it."

Then the LORD said to Satan, "Have you considered my servant Job? There is no one on earth like him; he is blameless and upright, a man who fears God and shuns evil. And he still maintains his integrity, though you incited me against him to ruin him without any reason."

"Skin for skin!" Satan replied. "A man will give all he has for his own life. But now stretch out your hand and strike his flesh and bones, and he will surely curse you to your face."

The LORD said to Satan, "Very well, then, he is in your hands; but you must spare his life."

So Satan went out from the presence of the LORD and afflicted Job with painful sores from the soles of his feet to the crown of his head. Then Job took a piece of broken pottery and scraped himself with it as he sat among the ashes.

His wife said to him, "Are you still maintaining your integrity? Curse God and die!"

He replied, "You are talking like a foolish woman. Shall we accept good from God, and not trouble?"

In all this, Job did not sin in what he said. (NIV)

A. What does this Scripture tell me about what God thinks about this topic?
- God thinks…
- God is…
- God…

B. What does this Scripture tell me about people?
- People are…
- People need to…
- People…

C. How do I apply this Scripture to my life today?
- I will…

D. Write out a prayer asking the Holy Spirit to empower you with strength to live out what He taught you today.

Grace Note:

This text shows you what's going on behind the scenes when we battle adversity, trials, and struggle. Job's life of faith is a beautiful example of how we are to deal with our hardship and adversity. If he can keep the faith in all his pain, we can keep the faith in ours as well. May it be said of us that in all our trials we did not give in to the temptation of blaming God or blaspheming Him! Let us praise Him regardless of what happens! He is good and His love endures forever!

What does God think about...

PARENTING?

Ephesians 6:1-4 *Children, obey your parents in the Lord, for this is right. "Honor your father and mother"—which is the first commandment with a promise—"so that it may go well with you and that you may enjoy long life on the earth."*

Fathers, do not exasperate your children; instead, bring them up in the training and instruction of the Lord. (NIV)

Deuteronomy 6:1-7 *"Now this is the commandment, and these are the statutes and judgments which the LORD your God has commanded to teach you, that you may observe them in the land which you are crossing over to possess, that you may fear the LORD your God, to keep all His statutes and His commandments which I command you, you and your son and your grandson, all the days of your life, and that your days may be prolonged.*

Therefore hear, O Israel, and be careful to observe it, that it may be well with you, and that you may multiply greatly as the LORD God of your fathers has promised you—'a land flowing with milk and honey.'

Hear, O Israel: The LORD our God, the LORD is one!

You shall love the LORD your God with all your heart, with all your soul, and with all your strength.

And these words which I command you today shall be in your heart. You shall teach them diligently to your children, and shall talk of them when you sit in your house, when you walk by the way, when you lie down, and when you rise up." (NKJV)

A. What does this Scripture tell me about what God thinks about this topic?
- God thinks…
- God is…
- God…

B. What does this Scripture tell me about people?
- People are…
- People need to…
- People…

C. How do I apply this Scripture to my life today?
- I will…

D. Write out a prayer asking the Holy Spirit to empower you with strength to live out what He taught you today.

Grace Note:
As parents, we are responsible to raise our kids to love God with all their heart and soul and mind and strength! We must make it the priority of our lives to raise our kids to walk with God. We can never take our stuff with us to heaven, but we can lead our children to walk with Jesus so they are in heaven with us someday. Parents, don't neglect the number one job you have: point your kids to Christ!

What does God think about...
PERSECUTION?

1 Peter 4:12-19 *Dear friends, don't be surprised at the fiery trials you are going through, as if something strange were happening to you. Instead, be very glad—for these trials make you partners with Christ in his suffering, so that you will have the wonderful joy of seeing his glory when it is revealed to all the world.*

If you are insulted because you bear the name of Christ, you will be blessed, for the glorious Spirit of God rests upon you. If you suffer, however, it must not be for murder, stealing, making trouble, or prying into other people's affairs. But it is no shame to suffer for being a Christian. Praise God for the privilege of being called by his name! For the time has come for judgment, and it must begin with God's household. And if judgment begins with us, what terrible fate awaits those who have never obeyed God's Good News? And also, "If the righteous are barely saved, what will happen to godless sinners?"

So if you are suffering in a manner that pleases God, keep on doing what is right, and trust your lives to the God who created you, for he will never fail you. (NLT)

A. What does this Scripture tell me about what God thinks about this topic?
- God thinks...
- God is...
- God...

B. What does this Scripture tell me about people?
- People are…
- People need to…
- People…

C. How do I apply this Scripture to my life today?
- I will…

D. Write out a prayer asking the Holy Spirit to empower you with strength to live out what He taught you today.

Grace Note:

Everyone who is a believer will suffer some sort of persecution. It identifies you with the suffering of Jesus! So don't get discouraged or stressed. You are blessed when you are persecuted. Just keep doing what is right, and honoring Jesus, and He will never fail you!

What does God think about...
PORNOGRAPHY?

Matthew 5:27-30 *"You have heard that it was said, 'You shall not commit adultery.' But I say to you that everyone who looks at a woman with lustful intent has already committed adultery with her in his heart.*

If your right eye causes you to sin, tear it out and throw it away. For it is better that you lose one of your members than that your whole body be thrown into hell.

And if your right hand causes you to sin, cut it off and throw it away. For it is better that you lose one of your members than that your whole body go into hell." (ESV)

Job 31:1 *I made a covenant with my eyes not to look lustfully at a young woman. (NIV)*

A. What does this Scripture tell me about what God thinks about this topic?
- God thinks...
- God is...
- God...

B. What does this Scripture tell me about people?
- People are…
- People need to…
- People…

C. How do I apply this Scripture to my life today?
- I will…

D. Write out a prayer asking the Holy Spirit to empower you with strength to live out what He taught you today.

Grace Note:
It's pretty clear here: to indulge lustful thoughts by looking at somebody you're not married to is the same as committing adultery with them. It's not just our actions that must honor God, it's also our thoughts and our words. So run from sexual temptation! Avoid things that cause you to look at pornography. Don't go near websites, TV shows, movies, apps, books, magazines, video games, etc. that will cause you to sin. You are called to a holy life because Jesus rescued you from the kingdom of darkness and set you on a better path in the kingdom of light. Stay away from all of the things that corrupt your mind and heart!

What does God think about...
THE POWER OF WORDS?

Proverbs 18:21 *The tongue has the power of life and death, and those who love it will eat its fruit. (NIV)*

James 3:1-12 *Not many of you should become teachers, my brothers, for you know that we who teach will be judged with greater strictness. For we all stumble in many ways.*

And if anyone does not stumble in what he says, he is a perfect man, able also to bridle his whole body. If we put bits into the mouths of horses so that they obey us, we guide their whole bodies as well.

Look at the ships also: though they are so large and are driven by strong winds, they are guided by a very small rudder wherever the will of the pilot directs. So also the tongue is a small member, yet it boasts of great things.

How great a forest is set ablaze by such a small fire! And the tongue is a fire, a world of unrighteousness. The tongue is set among our members, staining the whole body, setting on fire the entire course of life, and set on fire by hell.

For every kind of beast and bird, of reptile and sea creature, can be tamed and has been tamed by mankind, but no human being can tame the tongue. It is a restless evil, full of deadly poison. With it we bless our Lord and Father, and with it we curse people who are made in the likeness of God. From the same mouth come blessing and cursing. My brothers, these things ought not to be so.

Does a spring pour forth from the same opening both fresh and salt water? Can a fig tree, my brothers, bear olives, or a grapevine produce figs? Neither can a salt pond yield fresh water. (ESV)

A. What does this Scripture tell me about what God thinks about this topic?
    - God thinks…
    - God is…
    - God…

B. What does this Scripture tell me about people?
    - People are…
    - People need to…
    - People…

C. How do I apply this Scripture to my life today?
    - I will…

D. Write out a prayer asking the Holy Spirit to empower you with strength to live out what He taught you today.

Grace Note:
Your words create the atmosphere of your life. Just like God spoke the world into existence, you speak the atmosphere of your home into

existence with your words. If you speak positive words, the atmosphere of your home is beautiful and healthy. If you speak negative words in your home, the atmosphere of your home is destructive and discouraging. Make a commitment to not ever go negative with your words. Be an encourager. Cheer other people on. Don't whine or complain or gossip about others. Our words bring life and death, so be careful to speak life!

What does God think about...
PRAYER?

Luke 11:1-13 Once Jesus was in a certain place praying. As he finished, one of his disciples came to him and said, "Lord, teach us to pray, just as John taught his disciples."

Jesus said, "This is how you should pray:
Father, may your name be kept holy.
May your Kingdom come soon.
Give us each day the food we need,
and forgive us our sins,
as we forgive those who sin against us.
And don't let us yield to temptation."

Then, teaching them more about prayer, he used this story: "Suppose you went to a friend's house at midnight, wanting to borrow three loaves of bread. You say to him, 'A friend of mine has just arrived for a visit, and I have nothing for him to eat.' And suppose he calls out from his bedroom, 'Don't bother me. The door is locked for the night, and my family and I are all in bed. I can't help you.' But I tell you this—though he won't do it for friendship's sake, if you keep knocking long enough, he will get up and give you whatever you need because of your shameless persistence.

And so I tell you, keep on asking, and you will receive what you ask for. Keep on seeking, and you will find. Keep on knocking, and the door will be opened to you. For everyone who asks, receives. Everyone who seeks, finds. And to everyone who knocks, the door will be opened.

"You fathers—if your children ask for a fish, do you give them a snake instead? Or if they ask for an egg, do you give them a scorpion? Of course not! So if you sinful people know how to give good gifts to your children, how much more will your heavenly Father give the Holy Spirit to those who ask him?" (NLT)

A. What does this Scripture tell me about what God thinks about this topic?
   - God thinks...
   - God is...
   - God...

B. What does this Scripture tell me about people?
   - People are...
   - People need to...
   - People...

C. How do I apply this Scripture to my life today?
   - I will...

D. Write out a prayer asking the Holy Spirit to empower you with strength to live out what He taught you today.

Grace Note:
God wants to answer your prayers. God wants to give good gifts to His children, so ask, seek, and knock! Tell God what you need. He wants to come through for you. Heaven is waiting to move on your behalf. Pour out your heart to Him and let Him answer you.

What does God think about...
RACISM?

Galatians 3:23-29 *Before the coming of this faith, we were held in custody under the law, locked up until the faith that was to come would be revealed.*

So the law was our guardian until Christ came that we might be justified by faith. Now that this faith has come, we are no longer under a guardian.

So in Christ Jesus you are all children of God through faith, for all of you who were baptized into Christ have clothed yourselves with Christ.

There is neither Jew nor Gentile, neither slave nor free, nor is there male and female, for you are all one in Christ Jesus.

If you belong to Christ, then you are Abraham's seed, and heirs according to the promise. (NIV)

A. What does this Scripture tell me about what God thinks about this topic?
   - God thinks…
   - God is…
   - God…

B. What does this Scripture tell me about people?
- People are...
- People need to...
- People...

C. How do I apply this Scripture to my life today?
- I will...

D. Write out a prayer asking the Holy Spirit to empower you with strength to live out what He taught you today.

Grace Note:

There is no place in the Christian heart for racism. It is evil and wrong. God created all people equally in His image and likeness. Every race matters to God equally. We are to love people no matter what they look like or the cultural background that they come from, because Jesus died for all people. They are all His children and they all matter to Him.

What does God think about...
READING THE BIBLE?

Joshua 1:1-9 *After the death of Moses the servant of the LORD, the LORD said to Joshua the son of Nun, Moses' assistant, "Moses my servant is dead. Now therefore arise, go over this Jordan, you and all this people, into the land that I am giving to them, to the people of Israel. Every place that the sole of your foot will tread upon I have given to you, just as I promised to Moses. From the wilderness and this Lebanon as far as the great river, the river Euphrates, all the land of the Hittites to the Great Sea toward the going down of the sun shall be your territory. No man shall be able to stand before you all the days of your life. Just as I was with Moses, so I will be with you. I will not leave you or forsake you.*

Be strong and courageous, for you shall cause this people to inherit the land that I swore to their fathers to give them.

Only be strong and very courageous, being careful to do according to all the law that Moses my servant commanded you. Do not turn from it to the right hand or to the left, that you may have good success wherever you go.

This Book of the Law shall not depart from your mouth, but you shall meditate on it day and night, so that you may be careful to do according to all that is written in it. For then you will make your way prosperous, and then you will have good success. Have I not commanded you? Be strong and courageous. Do not be frightened, and do not be dismayed, for the LORD your God is with you wherever you go." (ESV)

A. What does this Scripture tell me about what God thinks about this topic?
    ▪ God thinks…
    ▪ God is…
    ▪ God…

B. What does this Scripture tell me about people?
    ▪ People are…
    ▪ People need to…
    ▪ People…

C. How do I apply this Scripture to my life today?
    ▪ I will…

D. Write out a prayer asking the Holy Spirit to empower you with strength to live out what He taught you today.

Grace Note:
God says He wants to make you prosperous and successful. He does this through your studying, reading, memorizing, and meditating on His Word daily. Don't take the Scriptures for granted. This is your life source for wisdom and making good choices. The more wisdom you have from God, the more likely you end up prosperous and successful. So read His Word every day!

What does God think about...
REPENTANCE?

Psalm 51:1-17 *Have mercy on me, O God, according to your unfailing love; according to your great compassion blot out my transgressions.*

Wash away all my iniquity and cleanse me from my sin. For I know my transgressions, and my sin is always before me.

Against you, you only, have I sinned and done what is evil in your sight; so you are right in your verdict and justified when you judge.

Surely I was sinful at birth, sinful from the time my mother conceived me. Yet you desired faithfulness even in the womb; you taught me wisdom in that secret place.

Cleanse me with hyssop, and I will be clean; wash me, and I will be whiter than snow. Let me hear joy and gladness; let the bones you have crushed rejoice. Hide your face from my sins and blot out all my iniquity.

Create in me a pure heart, O God, and renew a steadfast spirit within me. Do not cast me from your presence or take your Holy Spirit from me. Restore to me the joy of your salvation and grant me a willing spirit, to sustain me.

Then I will teach transgressors your ways, so that sinners will turn back to you.

Deliver me from the guilt of bloodshed, O God, you who are God my Savior, and my tongue will sing of your righteousness. Open my lips, Lord, and my mouth will declare your praise.

You do not delight in sacrifice, or I would bring it; you do not take pleasure in burnt offerings. My sacrifice, O God, is a broken spirit; a broken and contrite heart you, God, will not despise. (NIV)

A. What does this Scripture tell me about what God thinks about this topic?
   - God thinks…
   - God is…
   - God…

B. What does this Scripture tell me about people?
   - People are…
   - People need to…
   - People…

C. How do I apply this Scripture to my life today?
   - I will…

D. Write out a prayer asking the Holy Spirit to empower you with strength to live out what He taught you today.

Grace Note:

The word repentance means to change your mind or to change your thinking and go in a different direction. So in this text, to repent means to reject the ways of the world and selfishness and sin and instead embrace God and His wisdom. We ask God to forgive us for our failures and faults and ask Him to renew a spirit of faith in us! Every day, repent of the things that are anti-God and His will, and ask Him to forgive you. He always will because He loves you. The blood of Jesus covers all sin. Then turn from this sin and do the things that honor Jesus. This is true repentance.

What does God think about...
THE RESURRECTION?

John 20:19-29 *That Sunday evening the disciples were meeting behind locked doors because they were afraid of the Jewish leaders.*

Suddenly, Jesus was standing there among them! "Peace be with you," he said. As he spoke, he showed them the wounds in his hands and his side.

They were filled with joy when they saw the Lord! Again he said, "Peace be with you. As the Father has sent me, so I am sending you."

Then he breathed on them and said, "Receive the Holy Spirit. If you forgive anyone's sins, they are forgiven. If you do not forgive them, they are not forgiven."

One of the twelve disciples, Thomas (nicknamed the Twin), was not with the others when Jesus came. They told him, "We have seen the Lord!" But he replied, "I won't believe it unless I see the nail wounds in his hands, put my fingers into them, and place my hand into the wound in his side."

Eight days later the disciples were together again, and this time Thomas was with them. The doors were locked; but suddenly, as before, Jesus was standing among them. "Peace be with you," he said.

Then he said to Thomas, "Put your finger here, and look at my hands. Put your hand into the wound in my side. Don't be faithless any longer. Believe!"

"My Lord and my God!" Thomas exclaimed.
Then Jesus told him, "You believe because you have seen me. Blessed are those who believe without seeing me." (NLT)

A. What does this Scripture tell me about what God thinks about this topic?
- God thinks…
- God is…
- God…

B. What does this Scripture tell me about people?
- People are…
- People need to…
- People…

C. How do I apply this Scripture to my life today?
- I will…

D. Write out a prayer asking the Holy Spirit to empower you with strength to live out what He taught you today.

Grace Note:

If Jesus did not really rise again, then death is greater than God! But if Jesus really did rise again, then death has been defeated and the greatest God is Jesus! This is why Thomas says, "my Lord and my God." What is your response to the resurrection? Is Jesus your God? Is He your Lord? Like Thomas hit his knees and declared Jesus as Lord, will you hit your knees and make Jesus the Lord of your life also?

What does God think about...
SABBATH REST?

Exodus 20:8-11 *Remember the Sabbath day, to keep it holy. Six days you shall labor, and do all your work, but the seventh day is a Sabbath to the LORD your God.*

On it you shall not do any work, you, or your son, or your daughter, your male servant, or your female servant, or your livestock, or the sojourner who is within your gates.

For in six days the LORD made heaven and earth, the sea, and all that is in them, and rested on the seventh day. Therefore the LORD blessed the Sabbath day and made it holy. (ESV)

A. What does this Scripture tell me about what God thinks about this topic?
- God thinks…
- God is…
- God…

B. What does this Scripture tell me about people?
- People are…
- People need to…
- People…

C. How do I apply this Scripture to my life today?
- I will...

D. Write out a prayer asking the Holy Spirit to empower you with strength to live out what He taught you today.

Grace Note:

We rest because God rested on the seventh day. We have faith that we can get more done working only six days than we could if we worked all seven days of the week. We must have faith that as we rest, God is working! Our lives are not built on self-effort, but on His effort! So rest once a week, and tell God you trust that He is working on your behalf and He can get more accomplished than you ever could. Let Him work for you!

What does God think about...
SALVATION?

Romans 10:9-13 If you openly declare that Jesus is Lord and believe in your heart that God raised him from the dead, you will be saved.

For it is by believing in your heart that you are made right with God, and it is by openly declaring your faith that you are saved.

As the Scriptures tell us, "Anyone who trusts in him will never be disgraced." Jew and Gentile are the same in this respect. They have the same Lord, who gives generously to all who call on him.

For "Everyone who calls on the name of the Lord will be saved." (NLT)

A. What does this Scripture tell me about what God thinks about this topic?
- God thinks...
- God is...
- God...

B. What does this Scripture tell me about people?
- People are...
- People need to...
- People...

C. How do I apply this Scripture to my life today?
- I will…

D. Write out a prayer asking the Holy Spirit to empower you with strength to live out what He taught you today.

Grace Note:

Salvation is by grace through faith. The way our faith is expressed is we declare with our mouth that Jesus is Lord and we believe in our heart that God has raised Him from the dead. When we do this, we are saved! Notice here that it is more than just a heart choice, we make Jesus our Lord and Savior by speaking with our mouth! If you have never prayed aloud to receive Christ, do so now! Just say, "Jesus Christ, forgive my sins. Lead my life. You alone, Jesus, are Savior and God! Take me to heaven when I die and take me to my destiny as I live my life for You. In Jesus' name. Amen."

What does God think about...

THE SECOND COMING OF JESUS?

Revelation 19:11-21 *Now I saw heaven opened, and behold, a white horse. And He who sat on him was called Faithful and True, and in righteousness He judges and makes war. His eyes were like a flame of fire, and on His head were many crowns. He had a name written that no one knew except Himself. He was clothed with a robe dipped in blood, and His name is called The Word of God. And the armies in heaven, clothed in fine linen, white and clean, followed Him on white horses. Now out of His mouth goes a sharp sword, that with it He should strike the nations. And He Himself will rule them with a rod of iron. He Himself treads the winepress of the fierceness and wrath of Almighty God.*

And He has on His robe and on His thigh a name written: KING OF KINGS AND LORD OF LORDS.

Then I saw an angel standing in the sun; and he cried with a loud voice, saying to all the birds that fly in the midst of heaven, "Come and gather together for the supper of the great God, that you may eat the flesh of kings, the flesh of captains, the flesh of mighty men, the flesh of horses and of those who sit on them, and the flesh of all people, free and slave, both small and great."

And I saw the beast, the kings of the earth, and their armies, gathered together to make war against Him who sat on the horse and against His army. Then the beast was captured, and with him the false prophet who worked signs in his presence, by which he deceived those who received the mark of the beast and those who worshiped his image. These two were cast alive into the lake of fire burning with brimstone. And the rest were killed with the sword which proceeded from the mouth of Him who sat on the horse. And all the birds were filled with their flesh. (NKJV)

A. What does this Scripture tell me about what God thinks about this topic?
- God thinks…
- God is…
- God…

B. What does this Scripture tell me about people?
- People are…
- People need to…
- People…

C. How do I apply this Scripture to my life today?
- I will…

D. Write out a prayer asking the Holy Spirit to empower you with strength to live out what He taught you today.

Grace Note:
Jesus is coming soon! He will return in the clouds with His people. When He returns, He will crush evil and make all things beautiful and new. If you are not for Him, you are against Him. So trust Christ today! Choose the winning team!

1 Corinthians 6:12-20 *You say, "I am allowed to do anything"—but not everything is good for you. And even though "I am allowed to do anything," I must not become a slave to anything.*

You say, "Food was made for the stomach, and the stomach for food." (This is true, though someday God will do away with both of them.) But you can't say that our bodies were made for sexual immorality. They were made for the Lord, and the Lord cares about our bodies.

And God will raise us from the dead by his power, just as he raised our Lord from the dead.

Don't you realize that your bodies are actually parts of Christ?

Should a man take his body, which is part of Christ, and join it to a prostitute? Never!

And don't you realize that if a man joins himself to a prostitute, he becomes one body with her?

For the Scriptures say, "The two are united into one." But the person who is joined to the Lord is one spirit with him.

Run from sexual sin! No other sin so clearly affects the body as this one does. For sexual immorality is a sin against your own body.

Don't you realize that your body is the temple of the Holy Spirit, who lives in you and was given to you by God?

You do not belong to yourself, for God bought you with a high price. So you must honor God with your body. (NLT)

A. What does this Scripture tell me about what God thinks about this topic?
    ▪   God thinks…
    ▪   God is…
    ▪   God…

B. What does this Scripture tell me about people?
    ▪   People are…
    ▪   People need to…
    ▪   People…

C. How do I apply this Scripture to my life today?
    ▪   I will…

D. Write out a prayer asking the Holy Spirit to empower you with strength to live out what He taught you today.

Grace Note:
The Scripture here is clear that our bodies are temples of the Holy Spirit. What we do with our bodies matters to God. Therefore, sex must only be done in a way that is honorable before God. This means sex in any form

outside of marriage dishonors our body, dishonors God's temple, and is against the will of God. You must run from all sexual misconduct! The way that sex honors God is in the context of marriage between a man and a woman. In this context it is beautiful and wonderful and just another way in which a married couple can worship the Savior! Remember, in all things we wish to honor God, including with our sexuality.

What does God think about...
SHARING YOUR FAITH?

Matthew 28:19-20 *"Go therefore and make disciples of all nations, baptizing them in the name of the Father and of the Son and of the Holy Spirit, teaching them to observe all that I have commanded you. And behold, I am with you always, to the end of the age." (ESV)*

Romans 10:9-15 *...if you confess with your mouth the Lord Jesus and believe in your heart that God has raised Him from the dead, you will be saved.*

For with the heart one believes unto righteousness, and with the mouth confession is made unto salvation.

For the Scripture says, "Whoever believes on Him will not be put to shame." For there is no distinction between Jew and Greek, for the same Lord over all is rich to all who call upon Him. For "whoever calls on the name of the LORD shall be saved."

How then shall they call on Him in whom they have not believed?

And how shall they believe in Him of whom they have not heard?

And how shall they hear without a preacher?

And how shall they preach unless they are sent?

As it is written: "How beautiful are the feet of those who preach the gospel of peace, who bring glad tidings of good things!" (NKJV)

A. What does this Scripture tell me about what God thinks about this topic?
   - God thinks…
   - God is…
   - God…

B. What does this Scripture tell me about people?
   - People are…
   - People need to…
   - People…

C. How do I apply this Scripture to my life today?
   - I will…

D. Write out a prayer asking the Holy Spirit to empower you with strength to live out what He taught you today.

Grace Note:

The number one thing you can do before you die is lead somebody else to the Savior. In heaven you can never share your faith, so God left you here on earth now to share it so somebody else can be rescued from sin, Satan, and death! Speak up about Jesus. Talk about your faith wherever you go and whatever you do. Someone will give their heart to Christ if you just refuse to be silent. God wants to use you to bring good news to others!

What does God think about...
SIN?

Romans 3:10-23 *As the Scriptures say, "No one is righteous—not even one. No one is truly wise; no one is seeking God.*

All have turned away; all have become useless. No one does good, not a single one."
"Their talk is foul, like the stench from an open grave.
Their tongues are filled with lies."
"Snake venom drips from their lips."
"Their mouths are full of cursing and bitterness."
"They rush to commit murder. Destruction and misery always follow them. They don't know where to find peace."
"They have no fear of God at all."

Obviously, the law applies to those to whom it was given, for its purpose is to keep people from having excuses, and to show that the entire world is guilty before God.

For no one can ever be made right with God by doing what the law commands. The law simply shows us how sinful we are. But now God has shown us a way to be made right with him without keeping the requirements of the law, as was promised in the writings of Moses and the prophets long ago. We are made right with God by placing our faith in Jesus Christ. And this is true for everyone who believes, no matter who we are.

For everyone has sinned; we all fall short of God's glorious standard. (NLT)

A. What does this Scripture tell me about what God thinks about this topic?
- God thinks…
- God is…
- God…

B. What does this Scripture tell me about people?
- People are…
- People need to…
- People…

C. How do I apply this Scripture to my life today?
- I will…

D. Write out a prayer asking the Holy Spirit to empower you with strength to live out what He taught you today.

Grace Note:
This text shows us that all people are sinners and in need of a Savior. No one is perfect. No one is totally righteous without Jesus. That's why the phrase in the text is so important: "we are made right with God by placing our faith in Jesus Christ." Jesus' blood cleanses us from all sin and unrighteousness. We can be made holy and righteous and go from sinners to saints if we just ask Christ to forgive us our sins! Everyone is a sinner, but everyone can be made a saint if they would just trust Jesus.

What does God think about...

SPIRITUAL LEADERSHIP?

I Timothy 3:1-13 Here is a trustworthy saying: Whoever aspires to be an overseer desires a noble task. Now the overseer is to be above reproach, faithful to his wife, temperate, self-controlled, respectable, hospitable, able to teach, not given to drunkenness, not violent but gentle, not quarrelsome, not a lover of money.

He must manage his own family well and see that his children obey him, and he must do so in a manner worthy of full respect. (If anyone does not know how to manage his own family, how can he take care of God's church?)

He must not be a recent convert, or he may become conceited and fall under the same judgment as the devil. He must also have a good reputation with outsiders, so that he will not fall into disgrace and into the devil's trap.

In the same way, deacons are to be worthy of respect, sincere, not indulging in much wine, and not pursuing dishonest gain. They must keep hold of the deep truths of the faith with a clear conscience. They must first be tested; and then if there is nothing against them, let them serve as deacons.

In the same way, the women are to be worthy of respect, not malicious talkers but temperate and trustworthy in everything.

A deacon must be faithful to his wife and must manage his children and his household well. Those who have served well gain an excellent standing and great assurance in their faith in Christ Jesus. (NIV)

A. What does this Scripture tell me about what God thinks about this topic?
   - God thinks…
   - God is…
   - God…

B. What does this Scripture tell me about people?
   - People are…
   - People need to…
   - People…

C. How do I apply this Scripture to my life today?
   - I will…

D. Write out a prayer asking the Holy Spirit to empower you with strength to live out what He taught you today.

Grace Note:

As you read through this text, it sounds like church leaders have to be perfect, but there's nobody who could live up to this list except for Jesus Himself. So know this: God uses imperfect people. God uses people who could never totally live up to this list. God uses them all the time for His purposes. Don't be discouraged if you make a mistake on your journey to spiritual leadership. Do your absolute best to live honorably before God as spiritual leaders. However, if you make a mistake, ask God for forgiveness, move on, and do your best to point others to Him. Only Jesus could live out this list perfectly.

What does God think about...
SPIRITUAL GROWTH?

John 15:1-8 I am the true grapevine, and my Father is the gardener.

He cuts off every branch of mine that doesn't produce fruit, and he prunes the branches that do bear fruit so they will produce even more.

You have already been pruned and purified by the message I have given you.

Remain in me, and I will remain in you. For a branch cannot produce fruit if it is severed from the vine, and you cannot be fruitful unless you remain in me.

Yes, I am the vine; you are the branches. Those who remain in me, and I in them, will produce much fruit. For apart from me you can do nothing.

Anyone who does not remain in me is thrown away like a useless branch and withers. Such branches are gathered into a pile to be burned. But if you remain in me and my words remain in you, you may ask for anything you want, and it will be granted!

When you produce much fruit, you are my true disciples. This brings great glory to my Father. (NLT)

A. What does this Scripture tell me about what God thinks about this topic?
- God thinks…
- God is…
- God…

B. What does this Scripture tell me about people?
- People are…
- People need to…
- People…

C. How do I apply this Scripture to my life today?
- I will…

D. Write out a prayer asking the Holy Spirit to empower you with strength to live out what He taught you today.

Grace Note:
We must stay connected to Jesus to grow. He is the vine, we are the branches. Apart from Him we are unable to make progress, so stay connected to your Savior! Don't wander off and try to obey God on your own. We only make progress and bear fruit as we stay connected to Christ!

What does God think about...
SPIRITUAL WARFARE?

Ephesians 6:10-18 *Finally, be strong in the Lord and in his mighty power. Put on the full armor of God, so that you can take your stand against the devil's schemes.*

For our struggle is not against flesh and blood, but against the rulers, against the authorities, against the powers of this dark world and against the spiritual forces of evil in the heavenly realms.

Therefore put on the full armor of God, so that when the day of evil comes, you may be able to stand your ground, and after you have done everything, to stand.

Stand firm then, with the belt of truth buckled around your waist, with the breastplate of righteousness in place, and with your feet fitted with the readiness that comes from the gospel of peace.

In addition to all this, take up the shield of faith, with which you can extinguish all the flaming arrows of the evil one.

Take the helmet of salvation and the sword of the Spirit, which is the word of God.

And pray in the Spirit on all occasions with all kinds of prayers and requests. With this in mind, be alert and always keep on praying for all the Lord's people. (NIV)

A. What does this Scripture tell me about what God thinks about this topic?
- God thinks...
- God is...
- God...

B. What does this Scripture tell me about people?
- People are...
- People need to...
- People...

C. How do I apply this Scripture to my life today?
- I will...

D. Write out a prayer asking the Holy Spirit to empower you with strength to live out what He taught you today.

Grace Note:
When we became Christians, we chose sides in a spiritual war. There is an enemy out for our destruction. But don't lose heart - greater is He that is in you than He that is in the world! You stand your ground by putting on the armor of God. Each of these pieces of armor matter. So pray, put on the armor of God, and let God protect you from all the schemes of the evil one.

What does God think about...
TRANSGENDER?

Genesis 1:27-28 So God created man in His own image; in the image of God He created him; male and female He created them.

Then God blessed them, and God said to them, "Be fruitful and multiply; fill the earth and subdue it; have dominion over the fish of the sea, over the birds of the air, and over every living thing that moves on the earth." (NKJV)

A. What does this Scripture tell me about what God thinks about this topic?
   - God thinks...
   - God is...
   - God...

B. What does this Scripture tell me about people?
   - People are...
   - People need to...
   - People...

C. How do I apply this Scripture to my life today?
   - I will...

D. Write out a prayer asking the Holy Spirit to empower you with strength to live out what He taught you today.

Grace Note:

It is clear here that God made only two genders - male and female. We personally know and love many people who struggle with confusion regarding this issue. Please know if that is you, you are loved by God and the Scriptures can help give you clarity. Seek out a professional Christian counselor who can help you see yourself through the eyes of your loving Creator. It may take time to sort this all out. Please know you are loved, and God can give you clarity regarding these confusing issues.

What does God think about...
TRIALS?

James 1:1-8 This letter is from James, a slave of God and of the Lord Jesus Christ. I am writing to the "twelve tribes"—Jewish believers scattered abroad. Greetings!

Dear brothers and sisters, when troubles of any kind come your way, consider it an opportunity for great joy.

For you know that when your faith is tested, your endurance has a chance to grow.

So let it grow, for when your endurance is fully developed, you will be perfect and complete, needing nothing.

If you need wisdom, ask our generous God, and he will give it to you. He will not rebuke you for asking.

But when you ask him, be sure that your faith is in God alone. Do not waver, for a person with divided loyalty is as unsettled as a wave of the sea that is blown and tossed by the wind. Such people should not expect to receive anything from the Lord. Their loyalty is divided between God and the world, and they are unstable in everything they do. (NLT)

A. What does this Scripture tell me about what God thinks about this topic?
   ▪ God thinks…
   ▪ God is…
   ▪ God…

B. What does this Scripture tell me about people?
   ▪ People are…
   ▪ People need to…
   ▪ People…

C. How do I apply this Scripture to my life today?
   ▪ I will…

D. Write out a prayer asking the Holy Spirit to empower you with strength to live out what He taught you today.

Grace Note:

James says here we should consider trials an opportunity for joy because it gives our endurance a chance to grow. Eventually, we can be fully developed and lack nothing! Immature people cannot handle hard things. However, as we grow up strong in Christ, we can handle the difficulties of life and the things that the enemy throws at us. So don't lose heart in your trials! Don't give up! Say to yourself, "I will not quit. By God's grace I can do it!" You're going to make it through. The best is yet to come!

What does God think about...
WISE CHOICES?

Proverbs 1:1-7, 20-33 *The proverbs of Solomon the son of David, king of Israel: To know wisdom and instruction, to perceive the words of understanding.*

To receive the instruction of wisdom, justice, judgment, and equity; to give prudence to the simple, to the young man knowledge and discretion.

A wise man will hear and increase learning, and a man of understanding will attain wise counsel, to understand a proverb and an enigma, the words of the wise and their riddles.

The fear of the LORD is the beginning of knowledge, but fools despise wisdom and instruction. (NKJV)

Out in the open wisdom calls aloud, she raises her voice in the public square; on top of the wall she cries out, at the city gate she makes her speech:

"How long will you who are simple love your simple ways? How long will mockers delight in mockery and fools hate knowledge? Repent at my rebuke! Then I will pour out my thoughts to you, I will make known to you my teachings. But since you refuse to listen when I call and no one pays attention when I stretch out my hand, since you disregard all my advice and do not accept my rebuke, I in turn will laugh when disaster strikes you; I will mock when calamity overtakes you—when calamity overtakes you like a storm, when

disaster sweeps over you like a whirlwind, when distress and trouble overwhelm you.

Then they will call to me but I will not answer; they will look for me but will not find me, since they hated knowledge and did not choose to fear the LORD. Since they would not accept my advice and spurned my rebuke, they will eat the fruit of their ways and be filled with the fruit of their schemes.

For the waywardness of the simple will kill them, and the complacency of fools will destroy them; but whoever listens to me will live in safety and be at ease, without fear of harm." (NIV)

A. What does this Scripture tell me about what God thinks about this topic?
   - God thinks…
   - God is…
   - God…

B. What does this Scripture tell me about people?
   - People are…
   - People need to…
   - People…

C. How do I apply this Scripture to my life today?
   - I will…

D. Write out a prayer asking the Holy Spirit to empower you with strength to live out what He taught you today.

Grace Note:

The foundation of all wisdom is honoring God and respecting His thinking. The way to make wise choices in life is to seek His will in all you do. Study His Word. Seek out the thinking of Jesus regarding every issue. Wisdom is found in God alone! He will never let you down.

What does God think about...
WORKS AND GRACE?

Ephesians 2:4-10 *But God is so rich in mercy, and he loved us so much, that even though we were dead because of our sins, he gave us life when he raised Christ from the dead.*

(It is only by God's grace that you have been saved!)

For he raised us from the dead along with Christ and seated us with him in the heavenly realms because we are united with Christ Jesus.

So God can point to us in all future ages as examples of the incredible wealth of his grace and kindness toward us, as shown in all he has done for us who are united with Christ Jesus.

God saved you by his grace when you believed. And you can't take credit for this; it is a gift from God.

Salvation is not a reward for the good things we have done, so none of us can boast about it.

For we are God's masterpiece. He has created us anew in Christ Jesus, so we can do the good things he planned for us long ago. (NLT)

A. What does this Scripture tell me about what God thinks about this topic?
- God thinks…
- God is…
- God…

B. What does this Scripture tell me about people?
- People are…
- People need to…
- People…

C. How do I apply this Scripture to my life today?
- I will…

D. Write out a prayer asking the Holy Spirit to empower you with strength to live out what He taught you today.

Grace Note:
Salvation cannot be earned. You cannot achieve enough for God to let you in to heaven. Jesus already earned heaven for you. He already achieved the way to heaven. All you have to do is put your faith in Christ and ask Him to save you and His grace will save you! His grace is enough. Our work is never enough. So right now in this moment, ask Jesus Christ to save you through the work of the cross. He alone can bring you to salvation.

What does God think about...
THE WORLD'S SYSTEM?

1 John 2:15-17 *Do not love the world or the things in the world.*

If anyone loves the world, the love of the Father is not in him.

For all that is in the world—the lust of the flesh, the lust of the eyes, and the pride of life—is not of the Father but is of the world.

And the world is passing away, and the lust of it; but he who does the will of God abides forever. (NKJV)

A. What does this Scripture tell me about what God thinks about this topic?
- God thinks…
- God is…
- God…

B. What does this Scripture tell me about people?
- People are…
- People need to…
- People…

C. How do I apply this Scripture to my life today?
- I will…

D. Write out a prayer asking the Holy Spirit to empower you with strength to live out what He taught you today.

Grace Note:

You have to choose which side you are going to be on. You cannot love the world's system and the ways of the world and also love God. You're going to have to choose to follow God and His ways or the world and its ways. The world is passing away, but everyone who chooses Christ lives forever. Choose wisely. Reject the world and follow Jesus.

ABOUT ERIC DYKSTRA

Eric Dykstra is a pastor, teacher, and theology nerd. He and his wife Kelly founded Free Grace United, a family of churches in Minnesota, in 2004. Eric's passions include seeing people cross the line of faith and follow Jesus, bass fishing, and traveling with his family.

Eric is the author of *Grace on Tap* and *Unhooked & Untangled: Finding freedom from your addictions, vices and bad habits.* Both are available on Amazon.

His caffeinated teaching style engages even the most skeptical listeners and inspires people at all stages of faith. You can find his sermons at freegrace.tv.

Made in the USA
Monee, IL
15 July 2023

38760596R00098